WE ARE DISPLACED

MY JOURNEY AND STORIES FROM REFUGEE GIRLS AROUND THE WORLD

MALALA YOUSAFZAI

WITH LIZ WELCH

LITTLE, BROWN AND COMPANY
New York Boston

Copyright © 2019 by Malala Fund
Afterword copyright © 2021 by Malala Fund

Pages x–1, 42–43: map © Peter Hermes Furian/Shutterstock.com; pages 49, 69, 91, 99, 109, 137, 163, and 175: map © dikobraziy/Shutterstock.com; pages 81, 119, 151: map © pingebat/Shutterstock.com

Cover art: Geometric patterns © Lera Efremova/Shutterstock.com
Crowd of people © Angelina Bambina/Shutterstock.com
Cover design by Jaya Miceli and Neil Swaab
Cover copyright © 2021 by Hachette Book Group, Inc.

Little, Brown and Company
Hachette Book Group
1290 Avenue of the Americas, New York, NY 10104
Visit us at LBYR.com

Originally published in hardcover and ebook by Little, Brown and Company in January 2019
First Trade Paperback Edition: March 2021

Little, Brown and Company is a division of Hachette Book Group, Inc.
The Little, Brown name and logo are trademarks of Hachette Book Group, Inc.

The publisher is not responsible for websites (or their content) that are not owned by the publisher.

The Library of Congress has cataloged the hardcover edition as follows:
Names: Yousafzai, Malala, 1997– author.
Title: We are displaced : my journey and stories from refugee girls around the world / Malala Yousafzai.
Description: New York : Little, Brown and Company, 2019.
Identifiers: LCCN 2018043763| ISBN 9780316523646 (hardcover) | ISBN 9780316529488 (large-print hardcover) | ISBN 9780316523660 (ebook) | ISBN 9780316524315 (library ebook edition)
Subjects: LCSH: Refugees. | Forced migration.
Classification: LCC HV640 .Y685 2019 | DDC 305.23092/6914—dc23
LC record available at https://lccn.loc.gov/2018043763

ISBNs: 978-0-316-52365-3 (pbk.), 978-0-316-52366-0 (ebook)

Printed in the United States of America

LSC-C

Printing 1, 2021

no one leaves home unless
home is the mouth of a shark.

you only run for the border
when you see the whole city
running as well.

—Warsan Shire, "Home"

CONTENTS

CONTENTS

Prologue

Walking in the streets of Birmingham with my brothers, mum, and dad, I pause for a second to feel the peace. It is all around us, in the trees swaying gently in the breeze, in the sound of the cars coming and going, in the laughter of a child, in a girl and boy tentatively holding hands as they trail behind their friends. But I feel the peace, too, in my bones. I thank Allah for everything, for being alive, for being safe, for my family being safe.

It never fails to shock me how people take peace for granted. I am grateful for it every day. Not everyone has it. Millions of men, women, and children witness wars every day. Their reality is violence, homes destroyed, innocent lives lost. And the only choice they have for safety is to leave. To "choose" to be displaced. That is not much of a choice.

Ten years ago, before anyone outside Pakistan knew my name, I had to leave my home with my family and more than two million people from the Swat Valley. We had no other option. It was not safe to stay. But where would we go?

I was eleven years old. And I was displaced.

For any refugee or any person displaced by violence, which is what most often makes people flee, it seems as if there is no safe place today. As of 2017, the United Nations counts 68.5 million people who were forcibly displaced worldwide, 25.4 million of which are considered refugees.

The numbers are so staggering that you forget these are people forced to leave their homes. They are doctors and teachers. Lawyers, journalists, poets, and priests. And children, so many children. People forget that you were an activist, a student, that you were a father named Ziauddin, a daughter named Malala. The displaced who make up these staggering numbers are human beings with hopes for a better future.

I have had the immense privilege of meeting many individuals who had to rebuild their lives, often in totally foreign places. People who have lost so much—including loved ones—and then had to start over. This means learning a new language, a new culture, a new way of being. I share my story of being displaced not out of a desire to focus on my past, but to honor the people I've met and those I'll never meet.

I wrote this book because it seems that too many people don't understand that refugees are ordinary people. All that differentiates them is that they got caught in the middle of a conflict that forced them to leave their homes, their loved ones, and the only lives they had known. They risked so much along the way, and why? Because it is too often a choice between life and death.

And, as my family did a decade ago, they chose life.

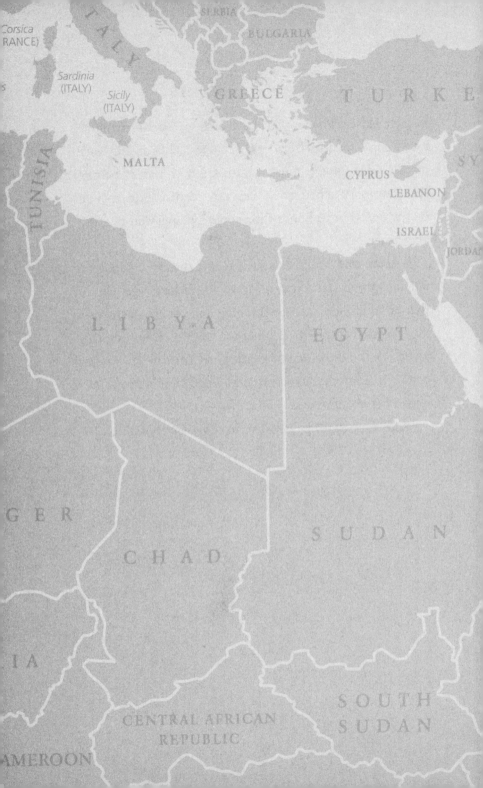

PART 1

I AM DISPLACED

CHAPTER 1

Life as We Knew It

When I close my eyes and think of my childhood, I see pine forests and snowcapped mountains; I hear rushing rivers; I feel the calm earth beneath my feet. I was born in the Swat Valley, once known as the Switzerland of the East. Others have called it paradise, and that is how I think of Swat. It is the backdrop to all my happiest childhood memories—running in the streets with my friends; playing on the roof of our house in Mingora, the main city in Swat; visiting our cousins and extended family in Shangla, the mountain village where both of my parents were born; listening to my mother and all her friends chatting over afternoon tea in our home, and my father discussing politics with his friends.

I do recall my father talking about the Taliban, but as a faraway threat. Even as a young child, I was interested in politics and would listen to everything my father and his friends discussed, even if I didn't always understand. In those days, the Taliban were in Afghanistan, not Pakistan. Nothing for us to be concerned with. Certainly nothing for me and my younger brother, Khushal, to worry about. And then came Atal, the baby. My biggest problem was how I felt about these brothers taking over the house.

That began to change in 2004. I was only six years old, so I didn't notice anything at first, but when I think back on those years, my memories are tinged with the fear that I know must have been growing in my parents' eyes. And then five years later, my beloved Swat was no longer safe, and we were forced from our home along with hundreds of thousands of others.

———

It started slowly. Our country had begun a time of advancement for women, but our region was going backward. In 2003, my father opened his first high school, and boys and girls attended classes together. By 2004, co-ed classes were not possible.

An earthquake in 2005 was not only devastating for the

destruction it caused and the lives it took—more than seventy-three thousand were killed, including eighteen thousand children—but it also left vulnerable survivors. When men from an extremist group who had provided aid to so many who had been displaced by this natural disaster began to preach that the earthquake was a warning from God, people listened. Soon those men, who later became part of the Taliban, began preaching strict interpretations of Islam on the local radio, saying that all women must cover their faces entirely and that music and dancing and Western movies were sinful. That men should grow their beards long. That girls should not go to school.

This was not our Islam.

These were religious fundamentalists who claimed they wanted to return to an old way of living, which was ironic considering that they used technology—the radio—to spread this very message. They attacked our daily way of life in the name of Islam. They told people what they could wear, what they could listen to, what they could watch. And most of all, they tried to take away the rights of women.

By 2007, the dictates had become more aggressive and specific: They called for TVs, computers, and other electronics to be not only banished from homes but also burned and destroyed. I can still smell the stench of melting plastic and wires from the bonfires they organized. They aggressively discouraged girls from going to school, commending by name parents who had kept their girls out of school as well as the girls themselves, and condemning by name those who had not. Soon they declared that educating girls was un-Islamic.

How was going to school un-Islamic? It made no sense to me. How was any of this un-Islamic?

My family mostly ignored these commands, though we did start lowering the volume on our TV in case anyone walking by outside could hear us.

The call for girls to be kept home upset my father, Ziauddin, too. He ran two schools that he had built from scratch; one was for girls. At first, these extremists still felt fringe to my father—more an annoyance than a real terror. He had been focusing his activism on the environment. Our city was growing quickly; air pollution and access to clean water had become problems. He and some friends had founded an organization to protect the environment as well as promote peace and education in the Swat Valley. He was becoming known by some as a man to be listened to, and by others as a troublemaker. But my father has a deep sense of justice and cannot help but fight for good.

Then the Taliban gained more followers and more power, and soon life as we knew it became a collection of happy memories.

The words *Taliban* and *militant* entered our daily conversations; it was not simply something discussed on the news anymore. And rumors were spreading throughout Mingora that these militants were infiltrating Swat Valley.

I began to see men with long beards and black turbans walking in the streets. One of them could intimidate a whole village. Now they were patrolling our streets. No one knew who they were exactly, but everyone knew they were connected to the Taliban and enforcing their decrees.

———

I had my first real brush with the Taliban on our way to visit family in Shangla. My cousin had several music cassettes in his car for the ride and had just inserted one into the player when he saw two men wearing black turbans and camouflage vests waving down cars ahead.

My cousin ejected the tape, grabbed the others, and passed them to my mother. "Hide these," he whispered.

My mother shoved them into her handbag without saying a word as our car slowed to a stop.

Both men had long beards and cruel eyes. Each had a machine gun slung over one shoulder. My mother pulled her veil across her face, and I could see that her hands were trembling, which caused my heart to beat more quickly.

One of the men leaned into the car and asked, "Do you have any cassettes or CDs?"

My cousin shook his head no, and my mother and I stayed silent. I worried the Talib could hear my heart thumping or see my mother's hands shaking. I held my breath when he pushed his face into the back window to address us both.

"Sister," he said sternly to me. "You should cover your face."

I wanted to ask, *Why? I am only a child.* But the Kalashnikov slung over his shoulder stopped me from speaking.

They waved us on, but all the excitement we had felt earlier that day disappeared. We spent the next hour in total silence. The cassettes stayed in my mother's purse.

The fear that had been growing around us now felt too close to ignore. And then the violence began.

CHAPTER 2

How Could This Be Happening?

I was eleven when the Taliban started bombing girls' schools throughout the Swat Valley. The attacks happened at night, so at least no one was hurt, but imagine arriving at school in the morning to find it a pile of rubble. It felt beyond cruel.

They had begun cutting our electricity and targeting local politicians. They even banned children's games. We had been told stories of Taliban fighters who heard children laughing in their homes and burst in to destroy the game. They also bombed police stations and attacked individuals.

If the Taliban heard that someone had spoken out against them, they would announce those names on their radio station. And then the next morning, those people might be found dead in Green Square, our city center, often with notes pinned to the bodies explaining their so-called sins. It got so bad that each morning, several bodies would be lined up in the town center, which people started calling Bloody Square.

This was all part of their extremist propaganda. It was working: They were asserting control over the Swat Valley.

My father had been cautioned to stop speaking out on behalf of girls' education and peace. He didn't. But he did start varying his routes home in case he was being followed. And I started a new habit: I would check the locks on the doors and windows before I went to sleep each night.

We felt hopeful when the army sent troops to Swat to protect us. But it meant the fighting had come closer. They had a base in Mingora near our home, so I would hear the whirring of helicopter blades cutting the thick air and then look up to see metal hunks filled with soldiers in uniform. Those images, just like Taliban fighters holding machine guns in the streets, became such a big part of our daily lives that my brothers and their friends started playing Taliban versus army instead of hide-and-seek. They would make guns from paper and stage battles and "shoot" at one another. Rather

10

than share idle gossip and talk about our favorite movie stars, my friends and I shared information about death threats and wondered if we'd ever feel safe again.

This was our life now. It was nothing any of us could have ever imagined.

Scary things became normal. We'd hear the big, booming sounds of bombs and feel the ground tremble. The stronger the tremor, the closer the bomb. If we didn't hear a bomb blast for an entire day, we'd say, "Today was a good day." If we didn't hear firearms being shot at night, like firecrackers, then we might even get a good night's sleep.

How could this be happening in our valley?

———

Near the end of 2008, the Taliban made a new decree: All girls' schools would be closed January 15, 2009, or they would risk being attacked. This was an order even my father would follow, because he could not put his students—or his daughter—at risk.

By then, I had begun to write a blog for BBC Urdu that later helped the world beyond our country learn our story and the truth of the attack on girls' education in Pakistan. I had written about how the walk to school, once a brief pleasure, had become a fear-filled sprint. And how at night, my family and I would sometimes huddle on the floor, as far away from the windows as possible, as we heard bombs exploding and the rat-a-tat-tat of machine guns in the hills surrounding Mingora. I missed the days when we had picnics in that same countryside. What was once our refuge was now a battleground.

Many girls stopped attending classes or left the area to be educated elsewhere when the ban was announced—my class of twenty-seven had dwindled to ten. But my friends and I continued going until the last day. My father postponed what would have been winter break so we could get in as much school as we could.

When the day came that my father was forced to close our girls' school, he mourned not only for his students but also for the fifty thousand girls in our region who had lost their right to go to school. Hundreds of schools had to close.

We had a special assembly at school, and some of us spoke out against what was happening. We stayed as long as possible that day. We played hopscotch and laughed. Despite the looming threat, we were children being children.

It was a sad day in our house for all of us. But for me, it cut deep. A ban on girls' schools meant a ban on my dreams, a limit on my future. If I couldn't get my education, what kind of a future did I have?

CHAPTER 3

Internally Displaced

Once what was technically our winter break was over, my brothers went back to school, and I didn't. Khushal joked that he wished he could stay home. I didn't find it funny.

The Taliban continued bombing schools. In my BBC blog post from only a few days after my school closed, I wrote, *I am quite surprised, because these schools had closed, so why did they also need to be destroyed?*

My father continued to speak out, and I joined him, appearing on TV and doing radio interviews. The ban on girls' education was so unpopular that the head of the Taliban was persuaded to soften it, and by February he had agreed to lift the ban for girls up to fourth grade. I was in fifth grade. But I knew this was my chance, so I pretended to be younger, as did some of my friends. For a few blissful months we attended what we called our "secret school."

———————

When peace between the army and the Taliban was declared not long afterward, we were relieved. But it never truly took, and the Taliban became more powerful. Things got so bad that on May 4, 2009, government authorities announced that everyone had to leave Swat. The army was planning to launch an intense military operation against the Taliban. They predicted full-fledged warfare, and it was not safe for people to stay in the valley.

My family listened to the news in shock. We had two days to evacuate.

My mother began to cry, but my father just stood there, shaking his head. "It will not happen."

All you had to do was go outside to see: It was already happening. The streets were flooded with people piled into cars and hanging out of buses. People were fleeing on motorbikes and trucks, in rickshaws and mule carts, all with the same wide-eyed look of shock. Thousands more fled on foot because there were not enough vehicles to go around.

Belongings were shoved into plastic bags, children were strapped to bodies and carried, and elderly people were pushed in wheelbarrows.

But my father refused to budge. He kept saying we should wait to see if this was real.

The tension in our house got so thick that my mother finally called my father's friend who was a doctor and said, "You must come quickly. This man is crazy. He is staying, and it is dangerous."

That same day, a relative came running to our home with the news. A distant cousin had gotten caught in the cross fire between the army and the Taliban. He was dead.

My mother started packing. We would go to Shangla the following day. We would become IDPs—internally displaced persons.

I am not an emotional person, but I cried that day. I cried for the life I was being forced to leave. I worried I would never see my home or friends or school again. A reporter had recently asked me how I would feel if I had to leave Swat someday and never return. At the time, I thought it was a ridiculous question, because I couldn't even imagine the possibility. Now here we were, leaving, and I didn't know when, if ever, we'd come back.

As my brothers begged my mother to take their pet chicks

(when my mother said they'd make a mess in the car, Atal countered with a suggestion that they wear diapers), I grabbed some clothes and packed a bag filled with schoolbooks. It was May, and our exams were at the end of June. I kept asking, "When will we be back? In a week? A month? A year?" No one could answer; everyone was too busy packing. My mother made me leave the books behind because there was no room. Distraught, I hid them in a closet and said a silent prayer that we would be home soon. She said no to my brothers, too.

Since we didn't own a car, we split up and squeezed into the already-full cars of two friends. I went with my friend Safina and her family, following right behind my father's friend, who took everyone else in my family. We joined the long queue of cars leaving Mingora that day. The Taliban had blockaded many of the streets, in some cases cutting down trees to do so, forcing traffic to only a few roads. The streets were so clogged and chaotic that we inched our way out of the city. At one point we passed a big truck that had a small platform joining its two front wheels. The platform was not meant for passengers, and yet I saw two people sitting there, gripping the hood as the truck made its way through the streets. Falling beneath the wheels of a truck was preferable to staying in Mingora. These were the choices people made that day.

no choice

16

From the relative comfort of our crowded car, I stared out in awe at the flood of people. Women with a bag on one shoulder, a child on the other. Some people with bags stuffed and weighing them down, others with nothing, not even shoes on their feet. I saw cars meant for five people packed with ten, trucks for ten packed with twenty. A woman with a scarf tied around the hands of her two daughters to make sure she didn't lose them in the crush.

What kind of choice was this? It was like a doomsday for our region. What we and all these people were doing wasn't a choice: It was survival.

The road we usually took to Shangla was barricaded by a large group of Taliban fighters, so we had to take a longer route that day. Evacuating civilians was the only chance the army had for defeating the Taliban without causing mass casualties. The Taliban knew that, and keeping us from leaving so they could have innocent human shields was their best course of action.

We made it as far as Mardan that first day, about seventy miles away. Camps were already set up, but we were lucky to stay with a friend of my father's. I remember little about that first night except for the fear and hopelessness I felt. My thoughts were a jumble of unanswerable questions: What will happen to us? Will our house be safe? Why has this happened? How is this our life now?

My father kept saying that this wouldn't last more than a few days and that everything would be fine, but we all knew that wasn't true.

In the morning we prepared to continue our journey to Shangla, and my father went to Peshawar. He had decided to stay there to work with three of his activist friends on pressuring the government to restore peace in Swat so all its residents could return home as quickly as possible. He wanted to be sure that people everywhere knew what was happening in our region.

As I hugged my father goodbye, I fought back tears. I had so many questions: When will I see you next? Will you be okay on your own? Will we be okay without you? But the words got balled up in my throat so that all that came out were great big sobs. I buried my face in my father's chest, trying to stifle my cries.

"*Jani*," he said, calling me by my pet name—it's Persian for "dear one"—"I need you to be strong."

After three days of uncertain travel, staying in the home of kind strangers one night and a dirty hotel the other, we had to walk the final fifteen miles, carrying all our belongings. We all just wanted safety and to see something familiar. To stop moving. I had never wanted to simply sit so badly in my life.

I was eleven years old—old enough to understand why we were fleeing. Atal was five, and he only understood that we needed to flee. But after a while, even my endless wondering ceased, and all I could feel was the same thing that Atal felt: exhaustion.

When we finally made it to the village, I let out the breath I felt I had been holding for days, since we'd first heard the order to evacuate. We were welcomed with open arms and pained faces. My uncle—my father's brother—was the first to speak.

"The Taliban were just here," he said. "We have no idea if they will be back."

My mother just shook her head, too tired to cry.

Nowhere was safe.

My uncle's house had stone walls, a wooden roof, and a dirt-packed floor. It smelled like the earth, woodsy and dank. I closed my eyes, trying to absorb the smell of mud, one of my favorites, because of what it meant. Home. Family. And at least for this moment, peace.

Chapter 4

Shangla

In Shangla, our family welcomed us. We moved back and forth between my mother's brother's and my father's brother's houses so we wouldn't crowd one house for too long. I liked staying with my uncle Ajab, my mother's brother, because on our first night, his eldest daughter, Sumbul, invited me to go to school with her.

I woke that first morning and got dressed for school, glad to do something that felt close to normal. That was when I realized the top I'd packed did not match my trousers. Sumbul smiled when she saw my dilemma and let me borrow one of her *shalwar kamiz*. Before, I may have teased her a bit about her country clothes, but on this day, I was grateful.

After breakfast, we set off, walking the half hour to school along a gravelly dirt road that continued up the mountain. I had so many questions about Sumbul's school, her friends, what her favorite class was. Despite worrying about when I'd hear from my father and what was happening back in Swat, I was excited that I could still go to school, especially since the reason I was there was because of the Taliban, who had forbidden girls to go. I liked that while I was forced to flee my own home because of their dictates, I could still defy them.

I joined Sumbul's class, even though it was a grade above mine, and was amazed to see that there were only two other girls in the room of more than a dozen boys. I was also shocked to see my cousin and the other girls cover their faces when the male teacher entered. I did not copy her. Neither she nor the other girls spoke throughout the lesson. They never raised their hands or asked questions. When we were excused for the first break, all the boys dashed out of the room in search of snacks or the bathroom. But the girls stayed put, talking quietly with one another.

I was in my own country, and with my family, and yet I still felt so out of place. I spoke too much and did not look down when the teacher entered the classroom. I wasn't being disrespectful; I was just being myself, not shy in a classroom, but always polite. I asked questions, like all the boys, but was the last to be called on.

On our way home, I asked Sumbul why she did not speak in class. She just shrugged, and I decided not to push her.

It was nice to be with family, but the reason was troubling. Would Mingora be recognizable when we returned? Would the Taliban retreat? Would the army succeed? What did that even mean?

Our days were the same for the next few weeks. I would go to school, come home with Sumbul, do homework or read or play with my cousins, and eagerly await news from my father. It was nice to be with my cousins—I had always loved being in Shangla—but this felt different. Usually my visits were finite. Now we had no idea how long we'd be staying.

My mother had a Nokia cell phone, but the service was so bad in the mountains that to get any connection she had to climb on top of a boulder in the middle of a field. She tried to call my father daily but was not always successful in getting through.

Finally, after about six weeks, my father told us it was safe to join him in Peshawar.

The trip from Shangla was not nearly as arduous—there were no army blockades, no Talibs waving us down—but we still could not get to Peshawar fast enough.

When we arrived, my father was waiting for us outside the home of the friend he had been staying with, arms outstretched, face beaming. He looked thinner but happy. Both of my brothers were bouncing in their seats, scrambling to see who could open the car door the quickest. We all rushed him in a group hug, and my tears, for once, were from happiness.

We were together; we were safe.

We spent the next several weeks moving around, relying on the generosity of friends and family. To be displaced, on top of everything else, is to worry about being a burden on others.

We had our IDP cards for food rations, like millions of others. Even formerly wealthy individuals who might have owned fields of grain now stood in line for a bag of flour.

I celebrated my twelfth birthday at an aunt's home in Haripur, our fourth city in two months. Although *celebrate* isn't the right word; nobody remembered it. (My cousin brought me a cake, but after midnight. It wasn't my birthday anymore. I knew they had all forgotten.) I had expected at least a small surprise, despite our situation, so I was disappointed. It seems silly now to think of poor little Malala, feeling sorry for herself on her birthday, while so many weren't even lucky enough to be in the comfort of a family member's home. I longed for the ease of my eleventh birthday, when I shared cake with friends. All I wanted was to return to Mingora, to go back to the home I knew before the Taliban. nostalgia

But I think I knew, even as a twelve-year-old girl, that the home I knew no longer existed except in my dreams. Still, even though there were no candles to blow out, I closed my eyes and wished for peace.

CHAPTER 5

Returning Home

When we received the news that we could finally go home, I felt almost numb. Sometimes you want something so badly that when it arrives, you wonder, *Is this real?*

As I climbed into the back seat of a family friend's red pickup truck next to my father, I thought, *Yes, this is real.* I was going home! Back to my own bed and books. To my friends and neighbors. To school!

But the drive home tempered my enthusiasm and sparked my anxiety. Along the route, we passed several houses pockmarked with bullet holes and others reduced to rubble. Signs of fresh warfare were everywhere, but it was otherwise serene. What were we returning to? Would it look like these villages we drove through? How long would it take to fix it all? The sun was shining, the sky a brilliant blue that outlined the clouds. Familiar waterfalls tumbled down rugged ravines, sparkling reminders of what Swat once was.

My father gasped as we neared Mingora and saw the Swat River ahead. I looked at his face, wet with tears, and understood why he was so overcome with emotion. I felt a tug at my heart. It was similar to the one I felt when I reunited with my father in Peshawar. I think it was hope.

I know now that that hope I felt at seeing my city again is something I was lucky to experience. So many people don't have even that. But that hope dimmed quickly, because the city I left was not the city I returned to.

———————

It had been almost three months since we left in a torrent of frantic people fleeing for their lives. And yet on our return, the streets were empty. No buses or cars or rickshaws. No people. It was so quiet that all you could hear was the rumble of the truck's engine above my father straining to contain his tears.

We rode in silence as we saw how our city had been

transformed. Nearly every building had been sprayed with bullets or reduced to rubble. Entire buildings destroyed. Burned-out cars abandoned in the middle of the street. But I also noticed that the masked men who carried the machine guns that wreaked such havoc were nowhere to be seen.

It broke my heart to see so much of my beloved Swat Valley so badly damaged, and my anger returned at having to flee in the first place, at the violence that had caused this.

When we arrived at our home, I was nervous. What if it had been bombed? We had also heard rumors of looting. What would we find? My father opened the front gate to our courtyard, where the grass now reached my knees.

The house was so still, and a bit dusty, but otherwise exactly as we had left it. Everything in its place. My brothers ran out to the backyard to check on the chickens and came back crying. They had starved to death. When I saw their tiny corpses, their bony feathers and wings entangled as if they had cuddled while taking their last breaths, I swallowed a salty sadness. I did not expect the chicks to survive, but still their downy skeletons felt symbolic of something much bigger.

I ran to the guest room closet: My bag of books was exactly where I had left it.

Overcome with emotion, I retreated to my bedroom to collect myself. We were home, my books were fine, the

Taliban were gone. This was all good news, I thought. So why did I feel so overwhelmingly sad?

———

Later that day, I went with my father to check on the school. Roads usually congested with traffic were empty. Our city, once filled with noise, was as quiet as a graveyard.

While our home was virtually untouched, it was clear the army had used the school as a base of operations. Desks were turned on their sides, and chunks of wall were blasted open, just big enough to fit the barrel of a machine gun. Paper was scattered everywhere, and a few cigarette butts had been stamped out on the floor. As we walked from room to room, my father kept shaking his head in disbelief.

In the days that followed, my dad contacted his staff. Everybody wanted to get back to work. People needed some semblance of normalcy. And there was so much to do to get there. We were back, but we had new challenges. We had returned to a war zone, and we were ready to start rebuilding—our lives and our city.

resilience

Being back in Mingora felt as if we had achieved victory. We were happy that there was finally peace, but we couldn't shake the lingering feeling that no one was safe, anywhere.

30

Before we were displaced, the Taliban fighters were out in the open, roaming the streets. Now they were in hiding and using targeted killings of people who spoke against them as their preferred form of terror. We couldn't see them anymore, but they were still fighting. Their men could be anywhere, at the market, outside a school, on a bus, but not in their familiar outfits. Their network had been broken, but they still existed in small pockets. The Taliban had not been destroyed; they had only been scattered.

————

Life returned to normal. The streets filled with taxis and rickshaws. Shops opened, as did schools and other places of business. We were readying our school to open and catching up with friends and neighbors. The tension we felt at knowing that the army had rid Swat of the Taliban but had not defeated them became part of our everyday existence, sometimes just a low hum of anxiety that was easy to ignore, other times, after news of an attack, a loud fear that was hard to drown out.

I went back to speaking up for girls' education. I had built a platform from all the media exposure I got while speaking out against the education ban and writing my blog, and I wanted to continue to use it for good. I had already started to see positive change. Four hundred schools had been destroyed (70 percent of them girls' schools), but many had been rebuilt. Things were getting better; even targeted killings had decreased. And we'd started to feel something like safety again. There was so much improvement that in time, even the low hum of anxiety faded, and we barely thought about the Taliban.

But life didn't go as planned. I had thought I would finish my education and maybe become a politician to help girls in Pakistan. Then on October 9, 2012, I was shot. I had been targeted by the Taliban for speaking out for girls' education and peace.

The story of what happened that day has been told and retold—I won't do that again here. All you need to know is that when you go through that kind of experience, there are often two extremes: Either you lose hope completely and you shatter and break into pieces, or you become so resilient that no one can break you anymore.

My life had once again changed because of a circumstance beyond my control. This time the violence was directed only at me, but it affected so many people in my life. I was moved within Pakistan for treatment, from Mingora to Peshawar to Rawalpindi, and then a week later, while still in an induced coma, I was flown to Birmingham, England.

I don't remember the attack, which is lucky, or anything about the week that followed. All I remember is being in the school bus, talking with my friends about our exams, and then opening my eyes in a hospital.

I was bruised, I had pounding headaches, and I had lost hearing in one ear and movement on the left side of my face. I was confined to a hospital bed. I was alone in a foreign city with doctors who seemed to know me but whom I did not know. I had once again become displaced. This time with machines helping to keep me alive.

And yet, I did not break.

CHAPTER 6

Caught Between Two Worlds

As I walked out of the hospital to start my new life—nearly three months after I was airlifted to England from Pakistan—the first thing I felt was a cold that cut through the purple parka someone had given me. It was two sizes too big, and I felt like a small doll. The frigid air crept down my neck and up my sleeves and penetrated my bones. I thought I would never warm up. The gray skies cast a subdued, almost gloomy effect on the white snow dusting the ground. I felt a deep longing for the warmth and sunshine of home.

We drove through Birmingham's streets to the high-rise building where my parents had moved after spending several weeks in a hotel. Birmingham's busyness reminded me a bit of Islamabad, although the skyscrapers here were so tall you got dizzy looking up at them. Some buildings lit up with neon signs that pulsed a rainbow of colors, while others looked as if they had been wrapped in tinfoil or shingled with mirrors.

The people were different as well—a mix of white and brown and black, European, Asian, and African. Women in burqas walked the frigid streets alongside women in miniskirts, goose bumps covering bare legs that ended in impossibly high-heeled shoes. I laughed to myself at the memory of seeing women not wearing headscarves in Islamabad and thinking that was liberal!

When my family flew to Birmingham from Pakistan, they arrived with only the clothes they were wearing. There was no time to go home, plus it was not safe. That meant they had to start from scratch in a world that was utterly foreign. Starting with our flat. My parents had to buy plates, pots, and cutlery so we could eat meals at home. In Pakistan, this would have made my mother so happy! She loved getting nice things for her kitchen in Mingora, but here she said that they did not feel as if they were hers. There was no sense of belonging—she felt like a stranger in a strange land.

It did feel as if we had landed on the moon—everything looked, smelled, and felt different. Just getting to our flat meant using an elevator. I had been in one the summer before with my father, so at least I had experienced being transported in a small metal box. But for my mother, it was like boarding a spaceship. She would literally close her eyes as soon as we entered and say prayers beneath her breath. And then once safely in the apartment, I would hear her speaking to herself. "We're on top of this building! What if there is a fire? Or an earthquake? Where would we go?" In Pakistan, we would just run out of the house. My mother liked being on the ground.

Those early days in Birmingham reminded me of being internally displaced in Pakistan—except the faces, the food, and the language here were foreign. We were comfortable; we were being well taken care of—but it had not been our choice to come here, and we missed home.

At first, I thought our stay in Birmingham was temporary. Surely, I would go home in time to take my exams in March. I didn't know threats were still being made against my life. My parents didn't want to scare me.

March came and went, and I missed my exams. But still, I would go back. Soon. And I would catch up with the other girls in my class. It was the same feeling that I'd had in the hospital, minus the fear of not knowing where my family was—that this was all temporary. Then I enrolled in a local girls' school in April. It started to sink in that maybe this life in Birmingham was mine now.

There was so much to get used to—starting with wearing itchy dark blue tights beneath my long wool skirt. I missed the comfort and ease of my *shalwar kamiz*! The school building was enormous—three stories made of stone—with three sets of stairs, red, blue, and green, which all led to different parts of various buildings that were connected with hallways and even bridges. It was a maze. It took me weeks to figure out my way around.

At least in the classroom, no one could tell how out of place I felt. It was impossible to fake it between classes and during study periods and at lunch. That was when I felt the most alone: I didn't know what to say to the other girls, who would sit together in clusters, giggling or rolling their eyes. I would pretend to read whatever book I had with me, missing Moniba, Malka-e-Noor, Safina, and all my friends back in Mingora in a deep way that gnawed at my stomach, like a hunger I could not feed. These girls in Birmingham seemed so different from my friends. Their mannerisms, the way they spoke, so quickly that all the words ran together. I did not know whether I should introduce myself and talk to them. Or should I wait to be invited? Should I laugh at their jokes? Should I tell a joke? They often used words I wouldn't use. Should I join in? Start swearing? Laugh when they laugh?

I was so exhausted from trying to figure it all out that I could not wait for the bell to ring, signaling the end of the day. At least at our new home, I could speak Pashto with my family and tease my brothers. I could Skype with Moniba and watch Indian soap operas with my mother. This was the only solace.

I still didn't accept how hard it was going to be for me to go back to Pakistan. By then, I knew the Taliban had publicly threatened me again, but in my young and hopeful mind, I knew I would go back. So even as I was growing more accustomed to it, I continued to hold on to the idea that Birmingham was temporary. Not the beginning of our life in exile. It was possible to both feel that it was temporary and somehow know that it was not.

One thing that helped was the thousands of letters I received from people all over the world, specifically from young girls and women thanking me for standing up for their rights. They reached me at a time when I was on the precipice of making a decision: to continue my fight for girls' education or not. That's when I realized the Taliban had failed in their mission: Instead of silencing me, they amplified my voice beyond Pakistan. People from all over the world wanted to support the cause I was so passionate about; they wanted to support me, and they welcomed me. That inspired me to continue my work.

From then on, whenever anyone asked, "What are your plans?" I'd reply, "To continue fighting for girls' rights to an education." I had begun my activism in Pakistan, and I would continue it here in my new home.

PART 2

WE ARE DISPLACED

I am not a refugee. But I understand the experience of being displaced, of having to leave my home, my country, because it has become too dangerous to remain. When I think of refugees and those who have been displaced, I think of resilience. Courage. Bravery. I think of the first trip I took to the Zaatari refugee camp in Jordan in 2014 and all the Syrians I met at the border. They had reached the end of their harrowing journeys but only the beginning of their new, uncertain lives. I think of Muzoon, María, and Marie Claire. I think of Najla and Zaynab. And these are just a few of the extraordinary girls and young women I have met who have inspired me to dig deeper into my own story of displacement to understand and share theirs.

Many people think refugees should feel only two things: gratitude toward the countries that granted them asylum and relief to be safe. I don't think most people understand the tangle of emotions that comes with leaving behind everything you know. They are not only fleeing violence—which is why so many are forced to leave, and is what's shown on the news—but they are escaping their countries, their beloved homes. That seems to get lost in the conversation about refugees and internally displaced people. So much focus is on where they are now—not on what they have lost as a result.

I am incredibly grateful to the United Kingdom for the warm welcome my family and I have received. But not a day goes by when I don't miss my home. I miss my friends and the taste of Pakistani tea that has been boiled with milk on a stove and sweetened with sugar. My mom makes rice and chicken here, my favorite dish, but it tastes different in Pakistan. I cannot explain it, other than to say it is tastier there. The same with our fish, which is thin and panfried with spices. Totally different from the deep-fried fish and chips everyone loves so much here in England. Everyone but me! I miss the sounds of Pashto being spoken in the streets and the smell of the earth after a heavy rain in the mountain village where my grandparents live. I miss the lush green of Swat Valley, the place I called home for the first fifteen years of my life.

But I don't miss holding my breath every time I saw Taliban soldiers in the streets of Mingora. Or checking and rechecking that our front door was locked throughout the night when I was ten, eleven, and twelve, when our valley was no longer safe. Nor do I miss waiting for my father to come back home at midnight after meeting with friends who opposed the

Taliban. My stomach clenches just recalling those dark nights I lay awake in my bed praying for his safe return.

I don't miss the sounds of my city under siege: the army helicopters whirring above our home or the bomb blasts that got louder and closer each day before the government finally forced an evacuation.

But I do miss home. And I recognize this mix of feelings in the stories of the girls and young women I meet. I never thought of myself as being a global advocate for refugees. When I go to a camp, I sit with people and ask them to tell me their stories. That's how this started. Me, listening. And they all have their own lists of sounds and smells and tastes they miss, people they didn't get to say goodbye to. They all have parts of their journey they'll never forget, and faces and voices they wish they could remember.

I've shared my story to honor the girls I've met. But now it's time to share some of theirs. Truth be told, I don't want to keep telling my story. My strategy in life is to live in the present and focus on the future, but I know people are interested, and if by telling my story I can take the light people shine on me and reflect it onto others, well, that is what I will do. I am part of this group of people who had no choice but to leave our homes. And together our stories span the globe even as they are grounded in our hearts.

Zaynab

Why Me and Not Her?

•

Yemen → Egypt → Minnesota

I met a powerful young woman in Minneapolis during a tour with the film about my life, He Named Me Malala. *We would screen the film for young people, and then I would talk to them afterward, asking them to tell me about their lives. While many girls told me their stories that day, one really stood out—her name was Zaynab. I could feel her determination. As it turned out, despite having been out of school for two years as she fled wars, Zaynab had just graduated from high school as valedictorian with a 4.0. Her sister, Sabreen, however, had a different experience. Not because she is not as bright or as determined. Zaynab got a visa and resettled in the United States. Sabreen did not have the same luck.*

—Malala

I still don't know why I got a visa to come to the United States and my younger sister did not. I was eighteen when I flew to Chicago. She was sixteen and left behind.

Saying goodbye to Sabreen in the airport in Cairo was painful. We had already lost so much. We'd left Yemen together two years earlier because it had become too dangerous to stay. We had lived with distant relatives in Egypt for two years while we waited for our visas. And there I was, getting on a plane to the United States—without her. That was December 2014. I have not seen my sister since. The missing I feel—of her, of Yemen, of the way things were before the violence—is so big, sometimes I think it might swallow me up.

And that feeling makes my experience as a refugee in the United States more bitter than sweet.

But I knew I was one of the fortunate ones: When I arrived in this country, I had a home to go to, even though it was one I had never seen before. Because when I arrived, I was reunited with my mother, whom I had not seen in fourteen years.

———————

My first day of school in Minneapolis was a Friday. I had been in the United States for only one week and did not speak any English. That morning was so cold that I wrapped my scarf around my face so only my eyes peeked through, and I still thought they might freeze into ice cubes. I had never been this cold in my entire life. I didn't know weather like this was even possible. The wind cut right through the new winter jacket my mom had bought me the day before. I was so cold that I thought my blood would freeze as I walked the short distance from the bus to the school. And I remember being so relieved to walk into that building—a warm welcome.

I was even happier to see so many Muslim students! My idea of the United States was that everyone was white, but then I saw a Somalian girl wearing a gorgeous green hijab, and another wearing one in bright red, then another in blue. It was as if a vibrant rainbow were streaming through the hallways.

When I went to the main office to get my schedule, I

felt a mix of excitement and intimidation. The school was huge and made up of several buildings. I did not know where any of my classes were—upstairs? down? this building or another?

I spotted someone who I thought could help me and gave him my schedule in desperation. He told me his name was Habib. I laughed, because that means "loved one" in Arabic, and it felt like a good sign.

Habib showed me to my first class, where my teacher introduced me: "This is Zaynab," she said. "She just arrived from Egypt." I didn't know what to say, so I said nothing.

Then a girl said, in Arabic, "So you speak Arabic?" and my heart, which had been clenched since breakfast, suddenly relaxed.

Her name was Asma. She was born in Somalia, where my mother was from, but had grown up in Egypt. And she stayed by my side that entire day. She was my guide and my translator, and she became my best friend. *selflessness*

I soon met a boy named Abduwalli. He was from Yemen but had left before the revolution, which meant he missed most of the bombings and death. He liked living in America and had no plans to go back to Yemen, which stunned me. I had been in this strange new place for only a week, and I could not imagine ever being as comfortable as Abduwalli seemed. I was also sure I would never stop missing Yemen.

———————

I was born in Yemen. My mother is Somalian, and my father Yemeni. He left us when my sister was born. I was two years old. I have no idea why he left or where he went—all I know is that he got married again. In Yemen, a man can have four wives. So he took another wife and left us to be with her.

I don't have many memories of my mom from Yemen. She left for the United States when I was around four years old. She got a visa through a lottery program and could not take us with her. I never missed her, though, or wondered why she couldn't take us with her because my father's mother raised us as if we were her children. We lived in Aden, one of the largest cities in Yemen. We had a big family. Lots of cousins, uncles, and aunts. The love my grandmother gave me and my sister was enough to make me not miss either of my parents.

Our grandma read to us and told us stories of our ancestors. She was so proud of our Arab heritage—we had a book of Arabic poems she would recite to us with a gleam in her eye. She was pure joy! My heart. So when she had a bad fall in September 2010, I was concerned. I was only fourteen, but I knew it was bad. She was in so much pain that my sister and I had to bathe and dress her, even feed her. She stayed in bed for a week but refused to go to the hospital. She insisted she was fine.

We believed her.

So I was surprised when I returned home late one evening, a few weeks later, to see people in our living room, all dressed in black. Some were crying. I smelled the coffee and saw that sweet dates were being served: This is what we serve when someone dies.

"What's going on?" I asked.

My aunt looked at me, her face slick with tears. She just shook her head.

Someone said, "She doesn't know?"

"Know what?" I was practically shouting. I knew that something terrible had happened.

I needed to know what.

I didn't want to know what.

Then someone said, "Your grandmother died this morning."

All the air was sucked from the room.

My grandmother was our everything. She played a major part in every dream I had for my future—the face I saw at my wedding, the one who would help me raise my children. Who else would teach me to give them the same love that she gave me and my sister? In all these dreams, my grandmother was with me, by my side, smiling. How could she be gone?

She was also the connecting piece to my father's family—without her, my sister and I were adrift. Meanwhile, things in Yemen were growing increasingly unstable, so my extended family started to scatter and disintegrate. Some cousins went with their parents to other cities in Yemen, while others fled to Europe. My sister and I stayed with our aunt, my father's sister. Her two daughters were older than we were and had also decided to flee. One had gone to Europe, the other to Syria.

We were living with our aunt in Aden when the revolution officially began at the beginning of 2011. It was influenced by uprisings in Tunisia that led to a regime change a few weeks earlier. Inspired by this result, activists in other Arab countries took note, and protests spread quickly—to Syria, Yemen, Egypt, and Libya. These Arab Spring protests demanded change. In Yemen, the people wanted our president, who had been in power for thirty years, to step down. The protests were peaceful at first, but the police started telling people that if they walked in certain areas, they risked being shot. That was when the anger boiled over. Stories circulated of innocent people being killed—even children coming home from school. When my uncle was shot on his way home from work, we knew no one was safe.

I was in class in early 2012 when I overheard two teachers talking about a bomb threat that had just been called in to our school. I thought, *This is it. We are all going to die!* The police arrived and deactivated it, thankfully. That is why I can tell my story.

No one knew who had called or what group had planted the bomb. The world was upside down. That moment marked the beginning of what news reports were calling "indiscriminate bombings." I called it bombs randomly falling from the sky with no one ever knowing when or where the next one would strike.

No one knew who was dropping the bombs because there were so many warring factions—the government, the revolutionaries, and the terrorist groups that wanted to take over the country.

One December morning, I woke up to the noise of explosions. My bed trembled with the entire building. I ran to the window and saw a cloud of dust and smoke rising in the air in the distance. I heard the crackle of stones falling and the desperate cries of people screaming.

Everyone in my house was awake by then, in shock.

"That could have been us," my aunt said.

Soon thereafter, I was awakened again by another big blast. This time our entire house shook violently. I felt a warm liquid seep across the sheets and glanced at my sister lying next to me. Her eyes were stretched wide, and I realized that she was so frightened that she had wet the bed. I was too scared to be mad at her. I ran to the window and saw that our neighbor's top floor was gone, disintegrated into a pile of rubble. Then we heard the screams, so close, so anguished, that I thought someone must be hurt or worse.

My aunt was still struggling with the death of my grandma—the added stress of these "indiscriminate bombings" made her even less stable. Something broke inside her that day. She started talking to herself and having these long crying bouts. She was supposed to be our caretaker, but instead, my sister and I had to take care of her. She did not seem connected to the reality of what was going on around us.

That was when I decided to contact my mom.

I had not spoken to my mom in years. Yet I knew she would help. When I finally talked with her, she told me to go to

Egypt, where my grandmother's second cousin lived. Many Yemeni people were fleeing—to Egypt, Italy, and Greece. Anywhere was better than staying in Yemen. The only place I had ever known, my home, had become too dangerous.

My mother said she would send money to buy tickets to Cairo. To be honest, I didn't want to go. I was afraid of an unknown future in a strange place. Yemen had become terrifying, but at least it was familiar. It was my home. It was also the last place I saw my grandmother alive. Leaving Yemen somehow felt as if I were leaving her.

As we packed for our journey to Egypt, I took all the last things my grandmother had touched, like her clothes, which still smelled like her. I took the Arabic poetry books I had won at a reading competition in school, as well as my own clothes, documents, and pictures. Finally, I folded up the quilt that had been on her bed, where she had died. It was the last thing she had touched. I could wrap it around myself if I ever needed a hug, I thought as I placed it in my bag.

We flew to Cairo, which was my first trip on a plane. I was scared but knew we had no choice. We moved in with a distant relative who lived in Barty in the Alf Mascan section of Cairo. I hated it there. It was dirty and smelled as if dead animals were rotting in the streets. *At least we would not be there too long,* I thought. My mother had been in touch with the US embassy, and my sister and I went together to apply for visas. Egypt was temporary.

Four months later, the embassy called me in for a health check. They did a bunch of tests and took some blood; the next time they called me in, they told me I had TB.

I said, "What's TB?"

I had no idea.

I had been coughing for two months straight and went through a period when I had a fever every night and would wake up in a cold sweat. I had stopped eating and lost a lot of weight, but when I went to the hospital to see why I was so sick, I was told it was no big deal. Nobody ever mentioned tuberculosis.

The house where we were staying had a computer, so I googled *tuberculosis* and learned that people can actually die from it. I had survived so much by then that to die from an illness felt particularly cruel. I told my second uncle, in whose house we were living then, what the embassy had said. I thought he would give me advice. Instead, he shouted, "Get out!"

"Why?" I said, stunned. "What have I done?"

"You're going to make us all sick!" He was screaming now.

He stormed around the house, gathering my things and throwing them at me. "Pack your things and *get out!*" he yelled.

I left the house in total shock. I did not even tell my aunt or sister what had happened, because I did not want them to get sick. Instead, I told them the embassy needed me to do more health tests. I told them I was going to stay at a nearby hospital. I lied. If they knew I had been kicked out, they would want to come with me, and I did not want to put them at risk.

It was hard to find a place to stay. In Egypt, a seventeen-year-old girl cannot rent a house by herself. People wondered, *Why are you alone? Whom will you be bringing back to the house each night? Are you a good or bad girl?*

Finally, I found a room in a house in the Aldoqqi section of Cairo. It was closer to the embassy, which was convenient because I had to go there daily for six months to get both pills and injections. The embassy officials needed to know I had completed my treatment before they would give me a visa. While the tuberculosis may have been subsiding, I started to feel sick from all the medicine. At least I was no longer contagious, so I went to see my aunt and sister, who had by then moved to another relative's house. I never told anyone how sick I really was.

I finished the treatment by mid-December, and the embassy said that I was finally approved to go to the United States. I was about to turn nineteen on December 27—this was the best birthday present ever.

"When do we leave?" I asked.

"Who's we?" the agent responded.

I said, "My sister!"

The agent looked perplexed and said, "I only have clearance for you."

The feeling of panic that started spiraling throughout my body was familiar.

I spelled my sister's name—S-A-B-R-E-E-N—and asked the agent to double-check her records.

I was sure they would find her paperwork. It would be approved. We would be fine.

The agent checked the computer and said, "I don't see anything in the system."

My heart sank.

Then she said, "Wait a minute—here she is."

I was so relieved. I knew it had to be a misunderstanding.

"Her application was rejected."

Those words were far worse than "You have TB." Not quite as painful as "Your grandmother is dead." But close.

"Why?" was the only word I could muster.

The agent shrugged and said, "All I know is that your application has been approved."

As I left the embassy that day, my head was full of questions: What had gone wrong? Did we make a mistake in the paperwork? Does she have some sort of sickness? Maybe I gave her TB? Why me and not her? And as I considered each scenario, I thought, *We can fix this. She will get approved. This is just one more obstacle.*

I called my mother first to share the shocking news. I could not even get excited that I had papers—my sister's not having papers negated that. My mom assured me it was a glitch. "We will work this out," she said.

Telling Sabreen was painful. She wanted to go to the United States even more than I did. When she was young, she was obsessed with the TV show *Hannah Montana*, and even before the troubles started in Yemen, she'd say, "One day I'm going to go to the US. That's where Hannah lives!"

She remained remarkably calm. No tears or even anger. Instead, she said, "I will be fine! I'll stay with our cousins and apply for another visa! I will come as soon as I can."

I held my sister tight and could feel the tremble in her body. She was fighting the same urge I was. If we both began to cry then, we might drown.

A neighbor drove me and my sister to the airport in December 2014. When I checked in, I was told I had to leave two bags behind. I had packed four—two big and two small.

They contained my entire life, but they exceeded the weight limit. The agent told me I needed to pay two hundred dollars to take them with me. I had twenty dollars, which I hoped was enough to buy food over the next forty-eight hours it would take me to get from Cairo to Minneapolis.

My flight was about to leave, and I had to decide: I left the heaviest bag with all my books and the journals I had kept since I was very young. I had wrapped them with my grandmother's quilt. That bag also had the only family photos I have of me and Sabreen as kids. I handed the bag to Sabreen and asked her to please keep it safe for me.

And then it was the time I was dreading. I had to say goodbye to my baby sister. Once again, she did not cry. Once again, I felt that deep tremble inside her bones, which matched mine. As we embraced, we whispered in each other's ear, "This is only temporary. I will see you soon."

"Maybe one or two months, tops," I said as I pulled away.

"Yes," she said. I could feel tears coating my eyes and tried to blink them away.

"I will wait for that."

Boarding that plane should have felt like freedom. Like hope. Like a dream come true. Instead, my heart felt like lead, heavy in my chest. I buckled myself in my seat and pressed my forehead against the window. I did not want anyone to see me cry.

———————

Once I got to the States, Sabreen and I stayed connected through FaceTime and were literally counting the days for her to join me. I told her about my new school and friends, the food, and how cold Minnesota was. She smiled at every detail, and we talked about all the places I would take her once she arrived—like the Mall of America! I had never been to such a place! With so many shops and different types of people!

Each time we spoke, however, her enthusiasm dimmed. We had not heard any news from the American embassy, and we were starting to worry.

After three months, Sabreen announced that she was tired of waiting. She had heard of refugees paying to have boats take them to Italy. She said she wanted to do that with a group of friends. She said that if she went to Europe, it would be easier for her to get her visa to come to America.

I had heard about the boats, too—and of people dying trying to cross the Mediterranean Sea. But my sister was adamant. She said, "I promise—this is going to be safe. It is a big boat. It even has bedrooms and a bathroom!"

She told me it cost two thousand dollars per passenger, so I thought, *Wow! It must be safe!* That was a lot of money.

My mom started saving—she was a nursing assistant and took overnight shifts to save up for the journey. She sent the money the following month.

And then we waited for news.

Sabreen

No Turning Back

•

Yemen → Egypt → Italy

I waited for Zaynab's flight to leave—I had to see it disappear behind the clouds before I could actually believe it was true. My big sister was gone. All I had was her oversized and heavy suitcase. I fought back tears as I dragged that bag through the airport and into the same car that had taken me there. My sister was in the air, flying to a new life, and I was returning to an old one. But different. From that moment on, everything felt so empty: the city, the house, my heart.

That first week was so hard. People treated me differently. When I was with Zaynab, I had support. She always had my back. Now, I was on my own.

I soon found a group of Yemeni girls that I befriended through my cousin Fahima. We all dreamed about leaving Egypt. One of them had heard about a boat that took people to Europe. We decided to investigate.

That was how I learned I needed $2,200: one hundred dollars would buy a ticket to the coastal city of Alexandria.

Once there, I needed another one hundred dollars to stay in a place until it was safe to travel. The remaining two thousand dollars was to board the boat to Italy.

When I told Zaynab I wanted to do this, she got quiet. "Isn't that dangerous?" she asked.

I was so disappointed—and a bit angry. Easy for her to say! It was better than waiting in Egypt for a visa that might not ever come. I was tired of waiting. It had been two years since I applied. So I begged my big sister to convince our mother it was a good idea. She promised she would.

I was so relieved when the money finally arrived.

The bus ride from Cairo to Alexandria was long. I sat with my cousin Fahima and two friends. We agreed to say that we were all sisters so we would not get split up. During that trip, I had to contain my excitement. After months of making plans and waiting for money to fund them, we were finally on our way. My friends and I talked about the ocean liner we were about to board—we imagined that we would get three meals a day and have a view of the water as we made our way to Italy. The person we paid for the trip had promised us this.

When we arrived in Alexandria, we paid the one hundred dollars for our accommodations and were looking forward to a good night's sleep. We had imagined a hotel room, so we were shocked when we arrived at an empty warehouse with a concrete floor and no furniture or even blankets. This was a mistake, we agreed as we all huddled together. The rest of the journey would be better.

After a cold and sleepless night there, we were ushered onto another bus. The windows had been covered by black plastic, which made it feel as if we were traveling at night, even though the sun shone brightly outside. While I could not see out the window, I knew from the bumpy and twisty ride that we were driving on backcountry roads. I felt a bit sick, mostly because the bus was so packed with people that there was no air to breathe. Then I overheard people talking about how dangerous the actual crossing was. "If we get caught, we will wind up in jail," I heard someone say.

That was when I got really scared. I knew what we were doing was risky, but I never imagined going to jail. For what? For simply wanting a better life? For wanting to be reunited with my sister? It seemed impossibly cruel, but as I listened to these stories in the pitch-black, I started to worry that I had made a mistake. If we got caught, and I went to jail, I would never see my sister again.

We traveled on that bus from 6 AM to 6 PM, but if anyone asked the driver to stop, he would ignore them. After a while, people were desperate. We needed to go to the bathroom! We needed water. At one point, passengers started shouting.

"Stop the bus!"

It worked—the driver slammed on the brakes, and the bus came to a lurching halt. I was so relieved! I needed to pee, and I was desperate for fresh air. Instead of opening the doors to let us out, the driver got out of his seat and stormed down the aisle, hitting people with his fist and shouting, "Shut up! If you make noise, you're going to get me arrested!"

That scared me so much that I forgot I had to pee. As he clomped back to his seat, he yelled, "This is not fancy travel! You're refugees. Shut up and stay silent!"

I closed my eyes to try to contain the tears leaking down my face. All my dreams of what this trip could be were crashing down around me. *We may be refugees*, I thought, *but he's treating us like wild animals.*

Everyone must have had similar thoughts, because the bus was quiet the rest of the trip.

An hour or more passed, and I was so parched. I just wanted to wet my mouth but had no water left. I was sitting with my friend, who went to get the water bottle from our other friend, who was sitting near the driver. Just as she got out of her seat, the bus stopped.

The driver opened the door, grabbed my friend and literally threw her off the bus, and shouted, "Run!"

Then he started screaming at everyone, "Go! Run!"

I jumped up and made my way to the door. I was holding my coat, which the driver grabbed and threw out the door, shouting, "Run, go! Run!"

My heart beat so fast that my feet could not keep up. I grabbed my jacket and started sprinting as fast as I could, following those running in front of me. And then I saw the never-ending expanse of blue. We were at the Mediterranean Sea. We'd made it.

As I ran toward the beach, I searched for the boat I had imagined—a big, fancy ship with sleeping bunks and toilets. Instead, I saw only three small fishing boats lined up on the shore. I was so confused. By then my lungs burned from running so fast. I started wheezing; there was not enough air for me to breathe in. Looking back, I now think that was panic I was feeling.

Where was the boat? We could not possibly be getting on the fishing boats in front of me. They were too small. The waves were too big.

I wanted to go back to my aunt's house. I did not want to get on one of those fishing boats to cross the Mediterranean

Sea. That was madness. And as all this dawned on me, I felt paralyzed—I literally couldn't move my feet.

At that moment, a man approached and asked, "Why are you crying?"

I said, "I can't go; I'm scared."

He said, "There is no turning back."

Selflessness But I could not move. Others were piling into the boats, and this man literally picked me up and placed me in one.

I snapped out of my daze and shouted, "My sisters! I cannot travel without them!"

He found them for me in the crowd. As they climbed into the boat with me, I felt much better. At least we were together.

Just then, our bus driver arrived brandishing a knife. He said, "Everyone who has any Egyptian money or jewelry, give it to me."

Everybody was confused. He started collecting our money and then saw a woman wearing a ring and said, "Give me that ring."

She did as she was told.

My friends and I were so scared that we started reciting the Holy Quran, asking Allah for help. This freaked out the man taking our money. "I have to do this to feed my family," he said. "I don't take any money from the travel fee—it goes to the big bus—and I make only a little bit of money. That's why I ask for your money—it is the only way for me to survive."

Someone mentioned his knife, and he said, "I don't have it to hurt people. I have it in case the police come while we are at sea. It is better to kill myself than be caught."

I knew then that there really was no turning back. My friends and I were already on the boat with other refugees, from Syria, Iraq, Somalia, Egypt. More were arriving as more buses pulled in. A mother approached our boat holding her five-year-old boy. She had to walk over slippery, wet rocks to get into our boat and lost her balance. The boy fell into the cold water. He did not cry, but when the two climbed into the boat with us, I noticed he was shivering.

I'd packed an extra jacket for the trip, which I dug out of my bag and gave to him.

We set off in rough waters, the waves crashing up and over the sides of our boat. I stayed huddled with my girlfriends and dreamed of the big boat with the bedrooms and bathrooms and three meals a day.

The man who had carried me to the boat was our captain. He assured us that we were going to a bigger boat, but that did not happen. We were in the middle of the sea when another small boat met us. He told us to get into it.

"Where is the boat with bunk beds we were promised?" I asked.

He said, "Once we get to the big boat, everyone will have their own room and a shared bathroom. There will be food."

But when we finally made it to the third boat, on the sixth day, none of that was true. While it was bigger than our fishing boats, it was made to hold only a hundred people, and there were four hundred of us. We had to squeeze ourselves on.

By then, we had eaten all the food we had brought with us and had been sleeping sitting up because there was no room to stretch out. Every morning, I would wake up after nodding off and see the sky and think, *Oh, am I in heaven? Am I still alive?*

———————

When I saw the third boat, I thought, *I'm not going to survive.* I was too exhausted to cry.

At least on that boat, they gave us beans, tuna, and bread. But the beans weren't cooked, and the bread was moldy. There was no bathroom, only a box where people could relieve themselves. It quickly filled, and every time the boat rocked, the contents would spill onto the boat floor, where we were sitting.

The captain told us we were getting close to the coast. But three hours from land, the boat ran out of fuel. Someone suggested swimming, but none of us had life vests, and I don't even know how to swim. I have never been so scared in my life.

After several hours of waiting for a miracle, someone saw a ship in the distance. People started shouting and crying.

It was a large ship, the one in my dreams.

The Italian coast guard looked for boats like ours because so many refugees were fleeing. That was what the sailors told us as they invited everyone on board. I have never been so thankful in my life. At that point, we had not had food or water for more than a day. That ship contacted the Red Cross, which sent another ship to rescue us. Meanwhile, the Italians gave us water and food and blankets. They let us use their bathroom, which was so clean that I burst into tears. Those tears continued all the way to Italy as the crew on the ship assured us they were taking us to a safe place.

Within two hours, I saw land for the first time in nine days.

I started to sob all over again. I never thought I would see land again. And yet, there it was in the distance.

Zaynab

Dream Big

•

Minnesota

We did not hear anything from my sister for over a month.

My mother was desperate.

"What if something happened with your sister?" she said.

I replied, "It's going to be fine!" But I was worried as well. I saw all these news stories about refugees who had drowned trying to make it to Greece or Italy. I couldn't let myself think it....

Finally, one night, I logged on to Facebook and saw a message from Sabreen.

I made it to Italy. I'm safe, it read.

I shouted for my mother to come see. Sabreen was alive! She'd made it.

She wrote back the next day to say that it was difficult to find Internet where she was staying and that she would call me as soon as she could.

Several months passed, and I found myself checking Facebook throughout the day, waiting for a message from Sabreen.

Every day I did not hear from her I was consumed with worry. I read so many terrible stories online about young refugee girls who were deported. Where would she go if that happened to her? Back to Yemen? There was nothing for her there.

I also read about sex trafficking—that became my biggest fear. One story told of a Syrian refugee who went to Europe, only to be put in a brothel and sold to men for sex. When I told my mother this, her face got pale. She had been on the phone with the US Embassy in Italy almost daily doing everything she could to get Sabreen to Minnesota. Nothing was happening. We felt so helpless.

The timing of our situation was terrible. The 2016 US presidential election had unearthed intense animosity against Muslim people in the United States. I had experienced this myself while I was shopping alone at the Mall of America. I was riding the escalator up when I saw a white man approach the top of the escalator. I was wearing my hijab, as I do everywhere, and this man stared at me and started shouting, "Jihad! Jihad!" I panicked, thinking maybe he had a bomb, and turned and ran backward down the escalator. He wanted people to think that just because I am Muslim I was dangerous. Meanwhile, I was terrified of what he might do to me.

My heart was pounding in my chest as I searched for somewhere to hide. I finally found the bathroom and locked myself in a stall. Behind the closed door, I slumped onto the floor and burst into tears.

Still to this day, I won't shop there by myself.

If it was this scary for me in Minnesota, what was it like for my sister?

———————

We finally got a message from Sabreen a few months later telling us she had been sent to a refugee camp in Holland. They had Wi-Fi there, which meant we were able to talk. It was so great to hear her voice! She was really okay! And so were her friends, who were in Holland with her. She introduced me to each of them. She sounded happy—so much happier than she had in Egypt. She sounded hopeful.

I did not know back then how harrowing her journey was. We did not talk of any details. Instead, we looked to the future and brainstormed ways to be reunited. We kept in touch through Facebook. We sent each other pictures. And then one day she called to say that she had met a guy from Yemen in the camp in Holland.

"He's nice," she said. "I like him."

I was like, *Okay! As long as she's happy, then I am, too.*

I was shocked when she called a couple of months later to say, "I want to marry him."

My stomach dropped. I said, "But you're not even eighteen! And you haven't even gone back to school yet."

She said, "He is going to let me go to school! Don't worry!"

She promised that she would get her education. And then she said, "I just want someone to be with."

That killed me.

Sabreen should be with me and our mother. She should be in school. She should learn things. Not on her own in a foreign country with no family. But who was I to judge her? My path was different.

That September, I started twelfth grade.

I was learning so much so quickly that my school let me skip tenth and eleventh grades. Earlier that year, in May, at the end of ninth grade, I had been introduced to the student council at our school. I loved the concept. It was totally new to me. We met in a classroom and talked about the issues we cared about.

One girl said, "We need to have more offerings at our cafeteria. We have so many people from so many different cultures. We should be more sensitive to that."

Another person said, "I think it is important to have more teachers of color, so we can see ourselves in our teachers."

I was emboldened by all these requests and decided to add my own. I wanted to know why there were no sports or activities for students: We did not have basketball or soccer or anything.

I loved sports, and back in Yemen, before the revolution, I had dressed like a boy so I could play soccer. Only boys were allowed to play, so I wore pants and big, baggy T-shirts and hid my hair in a hat. Soccer for me was pure happiness. So when I came to the United States, I was upset that there was no soccer at school. I mentioned it in May, and that September, when I moved to a new building for the twelfth grade, I was happy to learn it had a gym. One of my high school advisers said, "Okay, you talked about soccer, so start putting together your girls' soccer team!"

I recruited as many girls as I could. Many said, "But we've never played!" Some of the girls from Africa had never even kicked a ball.

I said, "That's fine! I can teach you."

I started training them. The uniforms were an immediate issue. Many of the girls were Muslim and had to be covered. So they played in their dresses until we could get long pants to wear under the shorts. We all covered our hair and resilience became the only refugee team in all of Minnesota.

At our first game, the referee said, "Who is your captain?"

We didn't have one, so my team said, "Zaynab, it should be you!"

I became the captain, and we went on to lose every game. Like 0–12. Just getting crushed.

But we did not care! We were so happy to play! And to learn all the rules. Our very last game, we lost 0–5. And we were so proud of ourselves! We played so hard! I was the goalie because ours finally gave up. Everyone was scared of that position—they were afraid of getting kicked in the face or badly hurt. That game, I caught something like forty balls.

A coach from the Homeless World Cup team saw me play and said, "You have to be on my team!"

I joined and played so hard that they gave me an award and invited me to play with the team at the tournament in Europe.

By then, my sister had moved to Belgium. If I went to Europe, there was a chance I could finally see her.

I had my visa ready and all my travel documents, but then President Trump announced the Muslim travel ban. I didn't have my green card yet.

I said, "I can't go."

In July, I was invited to a movie called *He Named Me Malala*. I went with a dozen friends from school, all refugees. After the film, we went to a lunch and were shocked when Malala walked in to join us. It felt as if we were meeting a movie star! But then she sat down and started asking us questions, and I realized, *She is just like us.* While our stories are different, I felt such solidarity with her.

During that lunch, Malala went around the table and asked, "What do you want to change?"

By then, so many of my dreams had come true—I had survived the danger at home. I had moved to America. I had graduated from high school and was planning to go to college. I wanted my sister to do the same, ideally with me, in the United States. And I realized in that moment that I had already changed so much. So had Sabreen—in ways I didn't know if I would ever fully understand.

Sabreen wound up marrying the man she met at the refugee camp. They have since moved to Belgium and live in an apartment. Her husband works in a shop, and my sister is studying Dutch. She says she is happy, and I want to believe her. They are expecting their first child in November 2018.

Sabreen still does not have papers. Which means that her child will be born a refugee. What does the future hold for Sabreen and her family? For me? For my country? My people?

I wanted to have a better life with all our family in

Yemen. I wanted my grandmother back. I know that these dreams are impossible, but I can make others come true by believing—in myself and in my goals. I want to finish my schooling so I can go back to that beautiful home and bring justice with me. I want to rebuild it. I believe that there can be a happy ending for every story, and I will create that happy ending for this part of my own story.

I dream big. I want my sister and anyone else who has gone through these hard times to dream big, too.

Muzoon

I Saw Hope

•

Syria → Jordan

At the Zaatari camp, one of our UNICEF guides told me about a young girl he wanted me to meet. Her name was Muzoon, and our guide said she was passionate about refugees getting an education in the camp. I had so many questions for her.

I met Muzoon in her tent, which she shared with her parents, two younger brothers, younger sister, and two other family members. It was cramped, but everyone was still so happy to meet me and my father, relieved to know that people cared what was happening to them.

Muzoon spoke very little English, but it did not matter. The sparkle in her eyes and the hope on her face shattered any language barrier. I felt a kindred spirit.

After the first meeting, I thought about Muzoon often. We lost track of her for a bit, and when I saw her again, her family had moved to a camp near Azraq. This time when I talked to her, we were in a room with other girls, and one of the younger ones said to me, "Malala, you are doing good work, but the girl who has changed my life is Muzoon." I smiled at this and encouraged her to go on. "I was going to be married off, but she convinced me to get an education. She has helped me follow my dreams."

People had started calling Muzoon "the Malala of Syria," but I knew she was the Muzoon of Syria.

—Malala

An aid worker told me that there was a girl who wanted to meet me. A girl who was fighting for the right to education. A girl who had suffered in this fight and had come through the other side.

When I found out the girl who wanted to meet me was Malala, I was ecstatic.

I had heard about her when I lived in Syria. I knew she was a real force and a person who was using her experiences to create change for girls across the world.

I knew that she had two young brothers and that her father was a teacher. We had a lot in common, and we had similar aspirations. I loved school, and I loved to dream about my future.

But when the war began in 2011, everything changed. There was no safety, no peace. The fighting got so bad— every day there were bombings, gunshots in the street. Schools were forced to close. We lived under siege for two years before my dad finally made the difficult choice to flee our beloved country.

He told me, "Even life in a refugee camp has to be better than this."

I didn't know anything about the camp, but we had no other options. I didn't want to leave my country. It was the the only home I'd ever known. But even at thirteen years old, I knew that if I did not leave then, it could be the end of my story.

Along with many others fleeing for their lives, we drove to the border and walked through the night. Unsure of what was ahead of us, we crossed into Jordan. When we finally arrived at the Zaatari camp, we were so thankful to have shelter: A twelve-by-twelve-foot tent became a makeshift home for me, my parents, siblings, and relatives. We were eight people living in such a small space, but at least we were all family. That was not the case throughout the camp, where strangers were often placed together.

Beyond a few sleeping mats, we had no furniture and no electricity. We had to walk a long way for water, which we used for drinking, cooking, and bathing. But I didn't worry as much about those challenges as I did about school—I was supposed to be in the ninth grade that year. If I did not continue studying, I could lose my chance to go to college. I could lose my chance of a future.

So I was relieved when I found out that the camp had a

school. And I was excited to start lessons and meet other students. Classes meant that I'd have a place to go every day and that even in this place, where everything felt uncertain, I could focus on achieving my dreams of learning and traveling the world. On the first day, I was shocked to see so few students in the classroom. It made no sense.

One day, I walked over to the recreation center, a place where people could go to play games or borrow books from the limited library. There, I saw a small group of girls my age. I walked up to the girls and asked, "Why are none of you in school?"

The girls laughed! One said, "Why bother?" They started talking about how their parents believed the best chance a young girl had was to marry. They said their parents believed that marriage was the best future for their daughters.

I knew this wasn't right. I knew that early marriage would trap girls in a cycle of poverty and deprivation.

I knew I had to do something about it.

I started going tent to tent, talking to people.

Another big obstacle was that so many people thought they would not be in the camp for long. They thought it was temporary, so they wanted to wait until they returned to Syria to continue their education. I understood that— no matter how accustomed to this new life I became, I felt unsettled every morning when I awoke to it. But I knew the only way through it was forward. I couldn't stand still and pretend it wasn't happening, and I wasn't prepared to sit back and watch others do the same.

I said over and over, "No one knows when we'll go back to Syria! We could be in the camp for years."

The truth is, many of those girls are still living there, stuck in limbo. And because the war has only gotten worse, many have lost hope.

One girl I met there stuck in my mind. She told me her family wanted her to marry a man in his forties, the age of her father. She was seventeen. I asked her what she thought about the arrangement. She shrugged and said, "What other future do I have?"

I heard in her question an openness, so I said, "If your family really loves you, they won't let you marry this man. Tell your father, 'If you really want to protect me, then let me go to school.'"

When I saw her a few days later, she ran up to me and said, "I am not going to be married! I am going to school instead."

I was so happy that I grabbed both of her hands. I said, "You and me, we can be the ripple effect. If we go to school, others will follow."

She squeezed my hands back and smiled. And in that flash, I saw hope.

Najla

Thousands of People,

Just Like Us

●

Sinjar, Iraq → Dohuk, Iraq

The Yazidi community is small, less than a million people, mostly concentrated in northern Iraq and parts of Turkey and Syria, but their cries for survival have now been heard worldwide. I had heard about Yazidi girls in the news and met with some in Dohuk, Iraq, who had been released by ISIS. Most of them couldn't speak, they were still so traumatized by their experiences. Who knows if those girls will ever recover from the horrors they endured. But Najla was filled with hope.

Najla had found a way out, which I learned was not unusual for her. When she turned fourteen, her family told her she could not go to school anymore because they wanted her to be a housewife, like so many other Yazidi girls. She refused and ran away to the Sinjar Mountains for five days to prove her point. When she returned home, her father was so angry that he didn't speak to her for a year. But he let her go back to school.

This is one of the first stories Najla told me when I met her, so I knew she was not only stubborn in the best way but also resilient. With her bleached hair dyed turquoise at the ends, she stood out. She asked me about hope that day and what to do when you lose

101

it. Najla has seen and endured so much in her young life. I know that she will always find her hope. It's why she was one of two girls I met during my Girl Power Trip in 2017 whom I invited to join me at the United Nations General Assembly that year. (Marie Claire, who you'll meet later, was the other.) "I don't want any other girl to go through the same as me," Najla told a roomful of world leaders. "Not all of them can fight as hard as I did."

—Malala

Even as a young girl, before the terrorists arrived, I always felt I was missing something.

I was born into a big family in Sinjar, Iraq, which is near Mosul, a large, diverse city in northern Iraq. I have eight brothers, five of whom are younger than me, and four sisters, all older. We are Yazidi, a small religious minority that is neither Muslim nor Christian.

When I was eight, I saw that many of my neighbors were going to school and I wasn't. I asked my parents, "Why am I not going to school like all these people?" They had no interest in girls getting an education, but my eldest brother fought for me and persuaded my father to let me and one of my older sisters go to school.

The first year in class, it was as if my eyes had suddenly been opened. The school was my door to see the world. When I finished primary school, my father would not let me go to secondary school. He said, "That's enough."

But it wasn't enough for me.

He wanted me to be a housewife, like other Yazidi girls

my age. It was not just my father, but the Yazidi community. They decided this together.

I was fourteen, and I knew I was smart. I wanted to be in school, so I ran away. It was all I could think to do. I stayed at a monastery for five days in the Sinjar Mountains. I knew I could not stay there forever, though. When I returned home, my father was furious and my mother frowned, but I know she was secretly proud of me. So were my sisters. They were so pleased because I was fighting for something I desperately wanted.

It was not easy to live for a year in a house where my father wouldn't speak to me, but I thought, *It's okay. We have time.* Eventually, with the help of my older brother Ismat, my father came around and let me go back to school.

I finished my first year of secondary school. But in 2012, my sister's husband, a soldier, was murdered. Immediately after that, my friend and neighbor burned herself alive on purpose. One of her brothers had heard that she had a boyfriend and told her father. She was so scared that she said there was no choice but death.

When I saw her run out of her home, engulfed in flames,

something broke inside me. I couldn't focus on my education at all. I was miserable.

I went back to school in 2013 and felt that I was becoming a whole person again. I was determined to finish secondary school and go to college.

But in August 2014, ISIS shattered those dreams.

We had heard stories about Daesh, another name for ISIS, kidnapping women and doing terrible things to them. Age did not matter. Children, old women. They targeted the Yazidis. They went to different villages and destroyed everything in sight. They took the girls and women and killed the men. They killed children, too. Some they buried alive. It was genocide.

We heard they took Mosul, which was less than two hours away. We still didn't believe they would come for us. But one night, as we were watching the news on TV, everything went black. Our village lost electricity, which was a bad sign.

People had already fled the village, worried that ISIS was coming. We worried they were right. We had tried to go to Dohuk, but ISIS controlled the streets. It was too dangerous. We were trapped.

That night, we slept on our roof. Two of my siblings

stayed awake because they were worried. When they saw lights in the distance, they woke us all. A stream of cars and tanks was headed our way. We could see the headlights poking through the darkness and hear the hum of engines.

We ran fast without shoes to our car, which we had packed for our escape. As we crammed eighteen people into one car, we heard the explosions and bullets and fighting getting closer.

We drove up into the Sinjar Mountains without headlights, the same mountains I had escaped to a couple of years earlier. My father was struggling to see, so I gave him directions while sitting on my sister's lap in the back seat. Another sister sat next to him, hyperventilating. She was so scared that she couldn't speak.

We spent eight days in the mountains. We weren't the only ones who fled their village. Thousands of people, just like us, were on the run. Some told stories of pretending to be dead, lying among their slaughtered loved ones and family members. We were lucky to be alive and together as a family. And we never went back home.

We next went to Dohuk, a city in the Kurdistan region, where Ismat worked for a hotel. We could not afford to stay at the hotel for too long, though, so we found shelter in an unfinished building—there were no windows or interior walls, just the concrete facade with rough spaces where we set up our temporary home. We lived there with more than one hundred families for six or seven months. I was happy because my family survived what we later learned was one of the worst Yazidi massacres. We met people who had lost all but one or two others in their family. We heard more stories of ISIS militants who kidnapped women, even girls as young as five. The more stories I heard, the luckier I felt—lucky to be with my family, lucky to be unharmed, lucky to be alive.

Soon I was lucky to meet Malala.

I had read about her and couldn't believe I was meeting her. I told her about my life and how I was teaching some of resilien the younger kids in the building to read and write because et I wanted them to have hope. She asked me what my dream was, and I said to go to college. But I admitted to her that I didn't know if I could, and I asked her for advice.

I said, "I'm a very strong person and confident. But if I lost my hope one day, what would I do? Where should I get my power again?"

She smiled shyly and said, "If you lose your hope, you will be able to look at yourself and what you have already accomplished. You are already powerful."

María

Nobody Can Take Away
What We Carry Inside

•

Iscuandé, Colombia → Cali, Colombia

In the summer of 2017, I traveled to Mexico and met many girls from Latin America who had been displaced because of organized violence. On that trip, I learned a new word: luchadora. It means "female fighter" in Spanish. While some luchadoras battle for glory, the girls I met that day were fighting for education and a better life.

María is one of those girls. She is also one of 7.2 million people displaced because of civil conflict in Colombia that has been going on for more than forty years.

Whenever María felt overwhelmed, she would focus on creating. When she was sixteen, she made a documentary about what it's like to be displaced because, she told me, she wanted people to see how displaced people live, "how displaced people struggle to push forward."

The day I met her, before we parted ways, she danced for us. It was brief, but all of us cheered and clapped, and as María smiled, I saw the joy as well as the determination and strength that keep her pushing forward.

—Malala

I wish I could feel my father. I have a hard time seeing him even when I close my eyes. My memories of him are hazy, like smoke.

I grew up near the coast in Colombia, in a rural area. My father was a farmer. If we wanted fruit, we just went out to our front yard and picked a mango from the trees. Or an orange or a *chontaduro*, a fruit native to Colombia. We had chickens and pigs and vegetables my mother grew in her garden. We had fields to run and play in. This is what I think of when I think of "home."

But we left when I was four, before many of those memories had a chance to take root. These images are based on my older siblings' and my mom's descriptions of what we lost. I think I remember, but I could be remembering only what I was told.

I can say the same about my father. My mom says I look just like him. We have the same round face and full cheeks, she says.

I don't remember his face that well, but I do remember the day we left the farm.

My older sister was eighteen. "Why do we have to leave?" she asked.

And my mom replied, "We have to go find work."

It was late in the day, and my father was nowhere to be seen. My mother seemed in a rush, and my sister asked, "Well, what about Dad? Where is he?"

My mother said, "He needs to stay here. He will join us later."

That same night, my mother and four siblings and I took a small boat to cross the river first. We were rushing, and that scared me. I did not know then that we were running away.

———

When we finally arrived in Cali, Colombia's second-largest city, my mother gave me a white stuffed teddy bear and said, "This is from your father." Her face was like stone.

What she wasn't telling me was this: My father had been violently killed just the day before, and we were running because my mother feared we were next. She kept that a secret from all of us for years.

We had nowhere to go in Cali. We wound up in a sprawling, makeshift camp, a city of tents fashioned from plastic sheets and any other garbage that could double as shelter. It was one of many informal settlements that had sprouted up because of the violence that had spread throughout the country.

I hated living this way. Even doing the simplest everyday things, like brushing your teeth or washing your clothes, was difficult since there were only two spigots for eight hundred people. My mother had to wait in a long line for water, for food.

I would ask, "But, Mom, why do we have to wait for this? Where are the mango trees?"

I didn't understand why we couldn't go back home. I didn't understand that we no longer had a home.

She explained that things were different now. We had to buy our food and needed money to do that, so she went tent to tent asking if people wanted to pay her to wash clothes.

Even at four and five, I felt the constant pressure of poverty, and the crime that comes with it—gangs ran the camp. Gunshots were normal, as was worrying about stray bullets. To make matters worse, we have darker skin than other people who live in Colombia and speak with a rural accent.

My family and I stood out, and people were horrible to us. We were treated worse than animals.

I understood what it meant to be displaced from a young age, though I did not know the word. It was not until we left that place, when I was seven, that my mom finally gave it a name. "We're displaced," she told me. The word was new, but the feeling was not.

My mother had learned it through a community organization for displaced families. They also helped us relocate—we moved to a house, and while it was better than a tent, it was so dilapidated that whenever it rained, water fell inside the house as well.

We did not complain.

Through the community organization, my mother joined a support group where people could share their stories with one another. And she enrolled me and my siblings in a theater program that met every weekend.

We did a play that all the kids wrote themselves, based on their own stories. Everyone in the group had arrived in Cali from different parts of Colombia, and each told his or her story of that journey. While we came from different places and backgrounds, our stories were similar in that we all had to leave or risk dying if we stayed. So we each told a piece of our story in a way that told the whole story of internally displaced people in Colombia. We called it *Nobody Can Take Away What We Carry Inside.*

Since that first rainy house, I have moved eight times. But I have never felt "at home" in any other place than the one I keep alive in my head, from when I was a child, before my whole world changed. Even though the government has declared the war over, the place I once called home is still considered guerrilla territory. It is still unsafe. Besides, we have been gone for so long that we are outsiders not only in Cali but there, too.

So when I dream of home, I dream of mangoes I can pick off the trees. I dream of quiet and grass. I dream of peace. And nobody can take that away from me.

Analisa

Lucky

•

Guatemala → Mexico → Texas → Massachusetts

While women and children all over the world flee wars and terrorism, there are some regions where the violence and oppression are within the community, or within the home. Analisa found herself in that situation and risked everything for what she hoped would be a better—and safer—life.

Like many before her, she found that escaping her life in Guatemala was only the beginning. The journey is so dangerous that not everyone who starts it survives. And yet, the number of people fleeing Central America—especially Guatemala, El Salvador, and Honduras—continues to grow rapidly. According to the United Nations High Commissioner for Refugees (UNHCR), nearly 300,000 people from the region sought asylum in 2017. Analisa made a decision that so many have and will continue to make. And once she made it, there was no going back.

—Malala

I t was dark.

We were nearing the last safe house on my journey when someone said Immigration had just been there the night before. My lungs tightened.

"If Immigration comes, just run as fast as you can and hide," our guide hissed. He had been yelling at us since he picked us up—"Hurry up!" "Be quiet!" "Stand still!" Treating us like animals.

Then the murmurs started: If Immigration caught you, you would go to jail and then be deported back to your country. If you were not caught, you would likely get lost and never make it to the United States.

I began to panic because I had no idea how to get back to Guatemala, either. I started to think I had made a mistake in coming.

———

Until I was four years old, I lived with my mother in a one-room house with no electricity in Mazatenango, a small city in Guatemala. She worked all day, selling flowers in the market, and then would stay out late at night. Basically, she was never home. My oldest sister took care of me, and my second-oldest sister took me to school with her so as not to leave me alone. There was never any food in the house. I remember being hungry all the time.

But then my mother died. She and my father had never been together, but he came to her funeral and took me back home to live with him and his wife. He thought my sister was too young to take care of me, and he worried that the father of my other siblings would treat me badly because I was not his.

When I celebrated my fifth birthday at my father's house, he made a cake for me. That was the first cake I'd ever had.

My father was playful and loving but also strict—after school, he wanted me to head straight to the market, where he had a sewing shop, to do my homework. He insisted that I always have good handwriting. When he checked my schoolwork, he would tease, "That number fell asleep!" if one of them was not perfectly straight.

My father started taking me to church. I was baptized Adventist. He taught me to respect others, to fear God, and to not get lost. By that, he meant he wanted me to live up to my potential. And unlike my mother, he never left me home alone. He had a motorcycle, and I went with him everywhere. Those rides made me sleepy, and he worried I would slip off the back of his bike, so he bought a yellow strap, which he tied around my waist to his.

He was my safety net.

I had just turned fifteen when my father had a bad fall—backward down a flight of stairs.

My half brother Oscar was visiting us at the time. I barely knew Oscar and did not really like him. My father wouldn't let us take him to the hospital, insisting he was okay, but when he started speaking and acting strangely, Oscar took him anyway.

My father never came home.

After he died, my stepmother went into deep mourning, and Oscar moved in. He took over the shop and my life. It was terrible: He did not want me to leave the house or go to work. I had plans to finish school and go to college to become a doctor, and I was saving money I earned at my father's shop to do that. Every Sunday, after I worked all week, my dad would give me ten quetzals. He told me to buy whatever I wanted—instead, I hid it under my bed. I wanted to save it for something big.

But one day Oscar found the money. He yelled at me, "Where did you get this?" I told him I had been saving it for many months, but he accused me of stealing from the business.

After he took the money, I realized I was trapped. This man I didn't know was not going to take care of me. Meanwhile, my stepmother, who was frail to begin with, had become quite ill. I think she was heartbroken.

I struggled with what to do—I knew I could not live in the same house with Oscar, but I had nowhere else to go.

That was when my half brother Ernesto called from the United States. He was my mother's biological son, but I didn't have any memories of him. He left Guatemala when he was fifteen, the same age I was at that moment. While my mother was still alive, she had not taken good care of him, either. He knew he was better off on his own. He learned of my father's death from my oldest sister, who was homeless and had no money to take care of me.

So Ernesto said, "Do you want to come live with me?"

I hung up the phone confused. I knew I could not stay with Oscar, and my stepmother was not well enough to care for me. On the other hand, I hardly knew Ernesto. He was my half brother, but so was Oscar. That did not mean anything to me. I asked God for guidance.

"Please send me a sign," I said.

It had not rained in a very long time, so I prayed: *If you send rain on Saturday, I will take that as a yes, that I should go and that you will protect me. If there is no rain, then I won't go. It will mean it is not worth the risk.*

That Saturday, for the first time in weeks, it rained.

The next time Ernesto called, I told him I was ready.

My stepmother was listening to my conversation. When I hung up the phone, she started crying. I promised her everything would be all right. I told her about the rain. I told her I had faith.

I told my friends I wasn't going to finish the school year because I was leaving. They kept teasing me that I would not remember them when I got to the United States. When I told my teachers, they laughed. No one believed I was actually going. It all made me sad.

I stopped going to school on a Tuesday and spent two days working at my father's shop. On Thursday, I bought new shoes that would last me through the trip. Then on Friday, all my friends came to my house. It finally sank in. As I hugged each of them and said goodbye, I fought back tears. They knew I was serious. My friend had been teaching me how to play guitar—he brought his and sang a farewell song for me. Then we sang it together.

When I went to say goodbye to my stepmother, we hugged, and she cried and said she would always pray for me. She was so ill by then that I worried more for her than for myself.

That night, Oscar said he was tired of taking care of me. I don't know why he was always so mad at me, but it made me all the more resolved to go.

The next day, I got on a bus to Petén, a region of Guatemala that borders Mexico. There, I spent the night in a secret house with five other people, all making the same journey. Two big guys, a Salvadoran woman, and two young guys around my age. We did not talk about why we were leaving. But I knew that each person felt, as I did, that there was no choice.

We were driven to the Mexico border, where we had to cross a river that is half in Guatemala, half in Chiapas, Mexico.

There, we got on a small wooden raft. The men who took us across had guns. "For the animals," they said. I understood when I saw crocodiles silently slipping off the shore and into the water. For the first time, I was truly scared. We were in the deep jungle—there were monkeys swinging above our heads in the trees and large rocks in the water we had to maneuver around. It started to rain, and I saw whirlpools ahead—we began to bounce in the rough water. People started to scream—if we hit a rock or were pulled into the current, the raft would sink. I closed my eyes and prayed for the hour it took to cross.

When the raft hit Mexican soil, I exhaled.

Once in Mexico, we climbed into a truck with twenty-five people from all over Central America. We learned that Immigration officials had been there the night before, so we had to be extra cautious. After driving on bumpy dirt roads for hours, we were ordered to walk across a hillside in the pitch-black. Finally, we arrived at a house that was under construction and were allowed to rest. I was so tired that I fell asleep. If someone had not wakened me, I would have been left behind.

We next squished into a small van that took us to another spot, where we had to get out and run to the next pickup point. That was chaos. Before the vehicle had even come to a full stop, more than one hundred people were being yelled at to get on as quickly as possible. I watched a little boy being thrown onto the truck bed as if he were a doll. A pregnant woman was crying as the men in charge shoved her and screamed. It was a cattle truck, and we were truly being treated like animals. There was not enough room for so many people, so I was pressed up against all these total strangers. We traveled like that for two days.

When we made it to the next safe house in Mexico, I opened my backpack. I was desperate for a shower and a change of clothes. I had packed two shirts, two pairs of pants, and some underwear. I saw that my stepmother had slipped in a small towel for me as well.

I was so glad to have it. I thought I would be in the United States within a week, but we got stuck in that village for an entire month. We were stuck because a truck, like the one we had just arrived on, had flipped over with immigrants inside. Many had died in the crash. Immigration was swarming the area, so we were told to lay low.

I feel really grateful that I was staying with good people. Our host had an iguana tattoo, so we called him Iguana. Five of us stayed with him, and he had a young son who would invite us to watch movies or play soccer. I was actually a bit sad when it was time to go because they were so kind.

When I reached the final leg of the journey, I started questioning whether I had made the right choice.

The man who met us near the Texas border kept threatening everyone in our group to keep quiet. He kept saying, "Stay calm!" but in a way that made everyone panic. He led us to the river and told us to leave all our belongings behind and cross with only the clothes on our backs.

I took a deep breath, begged God that everything would turn out okay, and then got on the raft. I was so close. But I'd heard lots of people say that crossing that river was particularly dangerous, the place where most were caught and deported before they even entered the United States.

There was no time to feel relief the moment our raft hit the shore—our guide told us to run as fast as we could. I was with two kids my age, a young mother, her three-year-old son, and an elderly woman. We all agreed to stick together.

We had been told to look for a small light by a bridge and to follow that, but there were so many small lights in the distance! We ran for two hours. The old woman struggled to keep up. She said over and over, "I can't."

I, too, was just about to give up when I saw the road ahead. By then, the old woman could barely walk. We were not on the road long when a police car pulled up. Several men in uniforms got out and made us kneel along the road. They shouted at us to take off our belts and shoelaces. Then they drove us to a gigantic warehouse, where they sat us all down on the concrete floor.

One of the officers kept yelling in Spanish, "Why do you do this? Do you like to suffer?"

He was the only person who spoke Spanish at the facility.

They took us to a room that was freezing—I learned that it was called the *hielara*, which is Spanish for "ice box." We were given aluminum blankets and told to line up to be counted and processed.

I was so tired I started to nod off, but a guard kept poking me awake. One by one, we were taken to be fingerprinted and weighed and to have our photos taken.

I was asked if someone in the United States would be responsible for me, and I told them about Ernesto. They asked for his number. I had memorized it, but I also wrote it on a patch in my pants, just in case.

Finally, they took me to a room and handed me the phone.

"Analisa?" It was Ernesto. "Are you all right?"

I assured him I was fine—just tired.

I did not have enough time to tell him I was a little relieved, too. To hear his voice. To have made it that far.

That same night I was put in a car and taken to a place called the *perrera*, which means "dog pound." Like the ice box, I don't know its official name. This was a gigantic warehouse that had chain-link fences separating different sections, so it felt as if you were a dog in a cage.

At least I was placed with other girls my age—the boys

were held separately. To distract ourselves, we compared journeys. "Did you cross by that place? What scared you the most? Did you meet any nice people along the way?"

One girl from El Salvador told me she had been traveling with another girl who did not make it.

"What happened?" I asked.

She told me they had come by train, which I knew was really dangerous. You have to leap onto the train as it is leaving the station or slowing down along the route. When her friend jumped on, she cut her leg badly. She bled so profusely that she died on the train. No one knew what to do. Someone panicked and threw her body out of the moving train.

The girl trembled as she told the story. She was still so traumatized by the experience, and I understood why: It was not the first time on my journey when I felt lucky to be alive.

I stayed two days in that place, I think. I am not sure, because the lights were so bright and there were no windows, so you couldn't tell if it was day or night.

I passed the time talking with other girls. I asked everyone how long they thought we'd be there. No one knew.

Others would cry, especially the little ones. The older girls and I would try to calm them down, but none of us knew what was going to happen.

We would just sit and watch as some girls got bracelets around their wrists or ankles; others had chains. No one knew why or who was next. Since we did not speak English—and none of the guards spoke Spanish—we did not know what they were saying. We would watch their body language and do our best to imagine what they wanted from us. It was impossible.

Finally, after five days split between the ice box and the dog pound, I was taken to a shelter with girls my age. I know now that these are children's shelters run by the Office of Refugee Resettlement. They're specifically meant for children who come here alone.

I liked it at first—I had a bed and could shower. I didn't mind that a whistle woke us every morning at six o'clock, like soldiers. We could go to classes to learn English and watch movies at night. But I felt impatient because I had no idea how long I would be there. Some of the girls I met had been there for six months, others for more than a year.

My brother, meanwhile, was doing everything he could to get me out of there. And after six weeks, he succeeded.

He was so happy to see me—I had made it! I was alive. But my mind was a blank slate. Everything was so foreign, including him. I had no memory of knowing him as a child, even though I knew I had. And this new place had so far been really unwelcoming.

But I know that no matter what happens, even with everything I have experienced and everything I will do, I am not alone, that God is always with me.

Before I left Guatemala, I asked God for a sign—and it rained. I also prayed that a church would be close to where I would live. I don't have my father, but I do have my faith.

When I arrived at my brother's house, I saw he lived behind an Adventist church. I looked up at the sky and thought, *Thank you, God.*

Marie Claire

A New Beginning

•

The Congo → Zambia → Pennsylvania

I met Marie Claire in a nondescript room in Lancaster, Pennsylvania. I had been invited to join an annual program there honoring the refugees and their host community. Lancaster is often referred to as the refugee capital of America, I learned, and though I had received the invitation a couple of years earlier, this was the first time I could make it.

My visit was a surprise to everyone there, and I gave a speech. That is just how it goes sometimes. I walk in, a surprise, and then I speak to a roomful of amazing people.

But always at events like these, I'm more interested in listening than talking. That day, I sat in that room with six refugee girls and boys, each telling his or her story. I remember Marie Claire not only for the story she told but also for the story she didn't. She was full of strength, but I could hear the pain in her heart and see the tears in her eyes. When she spoke, I felt her trauma as well as her triumph. The picture of this moment, as she revealed her past, is still in my head.

—Malala

My mother used to say to me, "Marie Claire, what do you want? You must follow your dreams!"

She first said this to me when I came home from school in tears because the other kids were so mean to me. I had arrived in Zambia the year before after escaping the violence in the Democratic Republic of the Congo with my family. I did not speak the language well or look like the other kids in my class. They would tease me, call me names, and even spit at me.

I would beg my mother, "Please! Do not make me go back."

And she would stroke my head as I cried in her lap and say, "Forget about them, Marie Claire! Follow your dreams."

I was thinking of those words when I woke up on June 16, 2016. The first thing I saw was my red cap and gown hanging on the outside of my closet door. I had placed it there on purpose the night before. I had to see it, to know that it was really happening.

I heard my father and siblings in the kitchen, and the clatter of breakfast dishes. He was speaking in a booming voice that filled the house with his pride.

This was a big day—and my dream realized: I was going to be the first person in my family to graduate from high school. My heart was full and cracked at once. This was my mother's dream, too. She should be here to experience it with me.

I was young when my family left the Congo—I don't know the exact age, and I don't have many happy memories of that time beyond playing with other kids in our village during the rare quiet moments between unspeakable violence. The war started the year I was born—it was all I knew. Mostly what I remember was running. We spent the first four years of my life living in the bush, literally on the run. I have hazy memories of heading south toward Zambia, always moving in the middle of the night and sleeping beneath thorny bushes during the day to protect ourselves from wild animals. I remember being hungry and tired and also knowing, at such a young age, that if we were caught by the militia groups terrorizing our country, we would be killed. And so we ran.

With the help of pastors and priests, we got a boat to Zambia. That was where many people were fleeing—the UNHCR states that even today, 4.25 million are internally displaced in the Congo and that more than six hundred thousand are refugees in sub-Saharan Africa. The war in the Congo is a civil war between rebel forces and the government, like the wars in Syria and Yemen. Although the Congolese war has been going on for much longer, people don't know much about it.

All I know is that my family was part of the constant stream of refugees fleeing the country in search of safety. We wanted to live. So we had to leave.

———

People in Zambia did not want us there. They would shout at us in the streets, "Go back to your country! Why are you here?" Kids would insult me and my siblings at school, even throwing rocks, shouting, "You don't belong here!"

We did not belong, but we had nowhere else to go.

My parents found a cheap one-room house for us, which was better than our tent made from plastic sheets we'd had at the refugee camp when we first arrived. Still, it was cramped—me, my two younger brothers, and two older sisters plus my parents meant eight people sleeping in one small room. We did not mind—it was much better than sleeping in the bush back in the Congo. Everything we had was better by comparison than what we'd left. My father kept saying it was temporary—he and my mother were saving for a bigger place.

In this new place, I could go to school for the first time ever. I was eleven. I started in grade three, and I was so much older and bigger than everyone else that all the other students laughed at me. I spoke no English and very little Nyanja, the local language in Zambia. Kinyarwanda, what we spoke in the Congo, was the only language I knew. Still, I understood the insults. The other kids knew I was a refugee. Like the people in the streets, they, too, would say, "Go back to the Congo! You don't belong here!"

Some of my teachers were mean as well, but a few supported me. They'd say, "You'll learn; it just takes time."

I was in third grade for two years. It was hard to make friends. My mom knew I was having a hard time at school. She, too, was having difficulty communicating. She got up every day and set up her table in our neighborhood and sold the things she grew and made to support our family. People would say horrible things to her or not want to pay. There was so much hatred. It reminded her of the Congo, what we had left behind. But where else could we go?

So whenever I said, "I'm not going to school today. The kids keep laughing at me; I can't take it," she would respond, "This is your life. Not theirs. Ignore them and focus on what you want."

What my mother wanted most was a better life for her family. She used to pray out loud, *Dear Lord, you can take my life as long as my children are safe.* We were still living at a refugee camp when she heard we could apply for refugee visas through the UNHCR. So when we moved to Lusaka, she found the office there and started the application process. She was told that it could take years. She was willing to wait.

We had no idea how long we would have to wait, but we did know we were not safe. We had already been attacked several times. Men wearing masks had robbed my mother one evening as she packed up her stand. Another time, they threatened my father, saying, "You had better leave, or we will kill you!" Resentment was brewing because my parents were making a decent living. We were not sure who those masked men were—they could've been from Zambia or the Congo.

One evening, we heard a commotion outside our house. More than ten men with machetes and knives had circled the building. Some banged on our door. There were robbers in Africa who would break into your house to steal stuff, but this was different.

My mother and father had heard of these vigilante mobs terrorizing refugees, and now one was outside our home.

I was twelve and paralyzed with fear. My siblings and I huddled in the corner as my mother shouted, "Do not take my children. If you must take someone, take me!" They attacked her first, dragging her from our hut into the street. My father tried to fight back as my siblings screamed and cried, begging them to stop. Then they turned on my father.

My mother died in front of us that day. The most painful memory for me is that she was left naked, something to this day I still can't understand. We thought my father had died as well. We watched as he was stabbed in the head several times.

———————

We went to go live with our older brother. We were in shock. At first, we thought both of our parents were gone. But after some days, the doctor told us that our father was alive.

A miracle.

The police came to interview us. They said they were looking for our mother's killers, but no one was ever charged. We didn't follow up because we were undocumented, which means technically we were not allowed to be in Zambia. We had no rights. We also had no mother. Or a home. I dropped out of school to help care for my father.

It took him months to recover, and for me as well. I could not have gone to school—it was all too much. I was in shock—it did not dawn on me until later, the brutal irony that we had escaped one violence for another. And I kept thinking of my mother's prayer, *You can take my life as long as my children are safe.* They took my mother, but not her love. I still have that, and it keeps me strong.

The year after my mother died, I rarely left home. My grief was overwhelming. When I was finally strong enough to return to school, my new teacher placed me in the sixth grade. I started taking school very seriously. It was a connection to my mother—she would always say, "Marie Claire, with a good education, you can do whatever you want." Neither she nor my father ever got the chance to go to school. It was her dream that I would go and graduate one day. So I studied hard, not just for myself but also for her.

Things got better as the years passed. I excelled at school;

kids stopped teasing me for being Congolese. I spoke the language fluently, and Zambia began to feel less hostile, more like home. We encouraged our father to remarry—I was busy with school, as were my siblings, and he seemed so alone. Through the pastor at his church, he met his wife, who is from the Congo as well. They married in 2012.

And then one day, my father got a call from the UNHCR saying our refugee application had been accepted. We did not learn where we were going—only that we would leave Zambia soon.

It was such bittersweet news—my mother had started the process so many years earlier. I remember that we got a call to be interviewed when she was still alive, and we were all so hopeful. But then we heard nothing for years—and in between we lost her. I was sixteen when they called us again: They wanted to interview everyone in our extended family who was applying. I was interviewed more than five times over the next three years. So when we got the call to say that we had been approved, I almost could not believe it.

One week before we were scheduled to leave Zambia, we were told that our new home was in Lancaster, Pennsylvania. I started to do some research and learned that it was the "refugee capital" of the United States because so many refugees lived there. I was excited—I was finally going to have papers. A home. A life. A new beginning. It started to feel real.

———

My guardian angel was Jennifer. She met me and my family at the airport when we arrived in Pennsylvania.

I will never forget seeing her standing there, this small white woman with a big smile and blond bangs, holding a sign that read, WELCOME TO LANCASTER! Since that moment, she, her husband, and their kids have become our American family.

I was almost nineteen and excited to finish high school. I had only one year left. But then I learned that at my new school, the cutoff was eighteen. I didn't want to do a GED, so I went to the high school counselor in charge of admitting students and asked him to please give me a chance. He explained that his experience with refugees was that so many had missed so much school by the time they arrived that it was very hard for them to catch up and become acclimated.

I convinced him I could do it—I was a good student and spoke decent English. I just needed a chance.

I kept imagining my mother whisper, *You can do whatever you dream.*

This was my dream.

When he said, "I will give you a chance," I held back tears.

He placed me in twelfth grade and told me I had five months to get my diploma. If I could not finish twelfth grade by June, I would have to do my GED.

Graduation was in June 2016. I woke up and saw my red cap and gown hanging in my bedroom. I heard the chatter of my family downstairs, in my new home. I jumped out of bed.

Six hundred people graduated that day, but I felt that I stood out, in a good way. I have pictures of my family carrying me on their shoulders through the crowds, their faces filled with joy. My father was smiling so hard his eyes were closed. Jennifer, whom I'd started calling my American mom, beamed with pride. As they threw me up in the air and caught me, I also felt my mother lifting me up in that airborne and suspended moment, smiling down from above.

Jennifer

I Needed to Do Something

·

Pennsylvania

My heart burst with pride and love on Marie Claire's graduation day. She was the first in her family to finish high school. This was a milestone for all of them, second to their arrival in Lancaster six months earlier.

Her graduation was a symbol of what was possible. Her family was so thrilled when she received her diploma that they began hollering in the otherwise quiet crowd. After the ceremony, they threw her up in the air, cheering. Other families looked at us as if we were crazy, but I didn't care.

I just thought, *You could not possibly understand what this achievement means to this family.*

In 2015, I was visiting my daughter to celebrate my granddaughter's first birthday, and reveling in the joy of being a grandmother, when I saw the photo of a Turkish police officer carrying the limp body of a three-year-old Syrian boy out of the Aegean Sea.

It struck me to my core.

I read that the boy's father, Abdullah Kurdi, was the only one in his family to survive. He, his wife, and two children had made it out of Syria and into Turkey, where they paid smugglers to take them across the Aegean Sea to Greece, but their boat capsized just off the Turkish coast.

As I read about the thousands of refugees fleeing Syria, I realized this was the biggest humanitarian crisis in my lifetime. And that I needed to do something.

That same day, I googled *refugee* and *volunteer* and found Church World Service (CWS), a faith-based organization that had a resettlement program in my own community, Lancaster, Pennsylvania. It was the first time I had ever heard of it.

When I returned home after helping my daughter, we had a little family discussion. I worked full-time, my husband traveled for work, and we had two teenage boys at home. I knew that if I was going to start volunteering, my family had to be on board. My children knew this might mean they didn't get the newest iPhone because a family we were helping might need groceries. Everyone agreed this was important. They each wanted to get involved.

———

Marie Claire and her family were the first refugees we were matched with when we started to volunteer that same month. All I knew was that they were being resettled from Zambia and were originally from the Democratic Republic of the Congo (DRC). I did not know yet that they had spent three years fleeing the Congolese war, literally on the run from violence. They finally made it to neighboring Zambia, where they spent many years, much of that time living in refugee camps, before getting asylum in the United States.

I couldn't speak to them before they arrived, and I wanted to understand as much as I could the circumstances they were fleeing, so I did my own research. That was how I learned that the Congolese wars, an extension of the lethal tensions between Tutsi and Hutus in Rwanda that spilled into the DRC in the early 1990s, were responsible for the deaths of approximately five million people—that's more than the entire population of New Zealand. Over 4 million are internally displaced, and there are approximately 445,000 DRC refugees in other nations. Learning the numbers and the history was not the same as understanding, but it did help me fill in some of the blanks.

My job was to meet them at the airport, drive them to their new home, and help get them settled. I took a vacation day from work because their arrival was in the middle of the week. My husband was in Texas and my kids were in school, so it was only me and a few other CWS volunteers.

When I first met the family at the airport, I was shocked by how thin most of them were. They were a group of four-teen people, including Papa, who was sixty-one; his wife, Uwera, Marie Claire's stepmother; and then their blended family, including Marie Claire; her sister Naidina, twenty-one; their brother Amor; his wife; and their three children, ages nine, five, and two. The kids especially looked so ema-ciated and sickly that I was concerned. And yet they had all dressed in their best outfits, the men in slacks and dress shirts, the women in colorful African dresses with their hair either wrapped in matching scarves or done in elaborate braids with beads. When I complimented them, Naidina said, "We wanted to make a good impression on our new country."

Marie Claire was extremely shy and cautious. She barely looked at me when she said hello.

As we drove to their new home, which the CWS found for them in a lower-income part of Lancaster, the family stayed quiet in the back, taking it all in. Meanwhile, I had a sink-ing feeling as I drove past houses that needed paint or had a sagging porch or had litter in the street. I wondered what the family was thinking, and then Naidina said, "Oh, this is so beautiful!" I was relieved to hear hope and enthusiasm in her voice.

We pulled up to the four-story city row house, and I took a deep breath. As we walked through the building, I took note of things that needed to be fixed, like the hole in the kitchen ceiling from the leaky bathroom above, and the scuffed walls in real need to be of paint. None of the windows had screens, and the small backyard was overgrown with weeds. There was only one bathroom for fourteen people. And the windows in the attic did not open—what if there was a fire and they had to get out?

Meanwhile, Marie Claire's family saw none of the flaws I worried about. They loved the house. They were completely overjoyed. In Zambia, they didn't have running water, let alone their own bathroom. They lit their homes with candles. They were overwhelmed, in fact, by how big the house was. I immediately understood the extent of my privilege: Where I saw so many problems, they saw opportunities.

I showed the women how to use the stove and refrigerator, since they had never seen either. I also showed everyone how to use the toilet and shower. While the kids ran up and down the stairs and fought over who got which of the five rooms, I learned that it was the first time anyone had ever been on an airplane and that no one had eaten in two days because the airline food was so foreign to them.

It was hard for me to leave them that day. They were overwhelmed, and I didn't know how else to help. I invited them to come to my house for dinner that weekend.

After giving them a tour of my home, Naidina and several others kept saying, "You have so much water!" At first, I was confused, but then I realized they were referring to our faucets. They were still floored that you could turn on the spigot and water would just appear. They had one bathroom in their new house, and I have several. It blew their minds. I learned that in Zambia they had to walk three days to get water.

On another afternoon visit, I made popcorn. They all gathered in front of the microwave in awe: They thought it was magic. They asked me to do it again, and all pulled chairs and stools around the microwave to watch.

Everything was new and delightful to them. It was a blessing to see my life through their eyes.

———

Marie Claire opened up slowly, and I began to see her determination. She made it clear that she wanted to go to an

American high school even though she was almost nineteen and already older than most seniors. Administrators at our local high school were not sure she could handle it. They were concerned that her studies in Zambia would not align with the course work here. Plus, her English was basic.

Marie Claire said to the admission officer, "Take a chance and believe in me."

And he must have seen the same determination that I saw, because he did.

I was nervous when Marie Claire started school that January. My son went to the local public high school and had a difficult time making friends his freshman year. But Marie Claire was not concerned with making friends or joining any clubs or teams. She was laser focused on her education and spent all her spare time studying and going to her English tutor. I know now that Marie Claire will likely succeed in anything she does because of that focus. She manifests realities for herself.

As much as Marie Claire and her family truly celebrate life, I've witnessed very low moments, too.

I bought Marie Claire and Naidina necklaces as gifts. I wanted to give them something special that they could

159

cherish. I also wanted them to have something they could wear always, to know that I was there for them no matter what. They were so moved that they started crying, sitting on my couch. At first, I thought they were happy tears, but I soon saw that my gift had touched a deep well of sadness in each of them. I asked them what was wrong.

Marie Claire spoke first.

"This is such a beautiful thing, all of this. Being here, with you, in the United States. But I just wish our mother were here to experience this with us."

They rarely talked about their mother, Furaha, but I knew by then the circumstances around her death, and I knew that both girls had witnessed it.

"She sacrificed her life so we could have this life." Naidina could barely say the words, she was crying so hard.

The pain I felt in my chest that day must be heartbreak: I wished their mother were there, too. I wished she could see what brave, strong, kind, determined, beautiful girls she had raised. But I also know that their mother's spirit carries on in each of her children, especially Marie Claire. She is unstoppable. She must get her determination and her moxie from her mother, as well as her tremendous sense of humility.

That deep grief is something the girls carry around with them. For every amazing accomplishment, their happiness is weighed down by the very real trauma that got them here. I imagine this is true for all refugees—the paradox of being grateful for a new life that is based on the painful loss of an old one.

Marie Claire referenced that pain when Malala invited her to speak during the youth session of the UN General Assembly in September 2017. I was in New York for the event and got to sit on the General Assembly floor, beaming proudly as Marie Claire shared her experience with the distinguished crowd of world leaders and diplomats, including the president of France, Emmanuel Macron.

Marie Claire looked calm and confident as she stood on that podium. Then she started to tell her story.

"One night, armed rebels broke into our house with the intent to take a life. We watched as our mother was killed. She sacrificed herself to protect me and my siblings." At this point in her speech, you could have heard a pin drop. Then more than ever, I wished her mom were still alive to see her daughter capture the attention of this entire crowd. But, of course, that is the irony: Marie Claire was there, at the UN, because of her mother's love and sacrifice.

Furaha should have also been the one to drive Marie Claire to college. To watch her settle on nursing as her major. She should have been at Naidina's wedding; she married another refugee she met in Zambia who had landed in Utah. They reconnected, and we were all in the wedding party and procession, another highlight.

Now, whenever I am with Marie Claire or any of her siblings, they introduce me as their American mom. I feel privileged and honored to have each of them in my life. The pride I feel in that title is at times overwhelming.

When Marie Claire arrived in America, she was so reserved and cautious. But I saw a spark inside her that was just waiting to become a blaze. With her, it really was an evolution. She was always focused and determined, but I watched as she grew more confident with support and encouragement. She not only embraces opportunities but manifests them. Only three short years ago, this young woman had an uncertain future—now she's fearless and unstoppable, making a real impact on the world. She ultimately wants to return to Zambia as a nurse and activist to help other refugees.

I know she will.

Ajida

At Nighttime, We Walked

•

Myanmar → Bangladesh

Starting in August 2017, thousands of Rohingya, a minority Muslim group in the majority Buddhist Myanmar, fled to neighboring Bangladesh. The Rohingya have long been mistreated, but a new wave of violence against them had begun. They were escaping Myanmar soldiers and extremists who call themselves Buddhist, who were setting villages on fire, raping women, and killing the Rohingya, who live primarily in the western Rakhine state, which borders Bangladesh. According to the UN, it was the fastest human displacement since the Rwandan genocide of 1994.

In September 2017, I spoke out against the tragic and shameful treatment of the Rohingya Muslims in Myanmar. Soon after, I met Jérôme Jarre at the Goalkeepers conference, an event hosted by Bill and Melinda Gates that celebrates progress toward eliminating poverty and disease around the world. Jérôme is a French activist and humanitarian who cocreated the Love Army with several of his artist activist friends to mobilize young people to respond to emergent world crises in a more direct way. Using social media to raise money, they had helped people affected by the 2017 Somali drought. After that effort, the Love Army raised money after a devastating earthquake in Mexico and then focused on Myanmar.

I have been so inspired by the work that Jérôme and the Love Army have done to help the Rohingya. I think often of the helpers around the world—people like Jennifer, who made it her mission to support Marie Claire and her family. But also the translators and the fund-raisers, people who donate five dollars or five hours to raise awareness. . . . All of this matters. All of this helps. Sometimes just being seen and acknowledged is enough to keep someone's spirits up. The work that Jérôme has done is help on a grand scale, mobilizing people all around the world to come together and support communities in need.

The Rohingya have been escaping persecution since the 1960s. The first refugee camp was set up in Bangladesh in 1990, where the numbers have since swelled to more than nine hundred thousand living in a no-man's-land of inhospitable mountains between Myanmar and Bangladesh that are prone to monsoons and floods. Once the Rohingya arrive there, they can't leave the premises or get work outside the camps. Bangladesh allows them to live on the land but not to integrate with Bangladeshi society. Muhammed, a Rohingya who works with the Love Army as a project manager, described it as an open prison.

Muhammed went to Bangladesh as a four-year-old in 1992. Now married, his son was born there in limbo. But Muhammed taught himself English, which helped him connect with the Love Army for Rohingya. While I have not visited Bangladesh, I knew I wanted to include a Rohingya woman's story in this book. And I knew that Jérôme and the Love Army would be able to help. With the money it has raised for the Rohingya displaced by violence, the Love Army has enabled and empowered them to build four thousand shelters and dig eighty-one deepwater wells. The money also funds three thousand Rohingya in the camps to do a variety of jobs ranging from construction to cleaning the camps to making clothes to acting as translators, like Muhammed, who helped Ajida share her story, and Ajida herself.

—Malala

When we first arrived at the camp, I had two feelings: relief, then confusion.

I was very happy we had made it to Bangladesh. My husband and children were alive. This felt like a miracle.

But the camp was not what I expected. It was just a big, open sky—no homes, only tents. We were given a plastic sheet and several bamboo sticks. As we set up our own plastic tent, I thought, *It could be worse. We could all be dead.*

I grew up in a small village in Noapara, in Myanmar, once known as Burma. My husband and I had a love marriage. We'd known each other our whole lives and realized we could read each other's mind. Eventually we fell in love. Sharing real love makes it much easier to live together. Many Rohingya have an arranged marriage, but then you don't know the person or if it will work out. My husband and I were fortunate. I was fifteen when I married him, and now we have three children together, ages nine, seven, and four.

Around midnight one night almost two years ago, the big sounds of guns woke us. The military and the police had surrounded our village and were setting fire to every house. We had heard the military was coming through villages, raping women and young girls and killing the men. Terrified they were going to do the same to us, we grabbed our children and ran into the forest, lucky to escape. We learned later that my husband's brother was killed along with many of our neighbors.

We stayed in the forest for several days. We thought we could return after the military left but learned that was not possible. So many people had been killed, and everything had been destroyed.

Then we learned that the army had not left the area. We knew if we returned to our village, they would kill all of us.

We had no choice but to run.

We had nothing—no food, just the clothes on our backs. My children were crying from hunger. I fed them green leaves from the jungle. There was nothing else. We were with a group of more than three hundred people from our village and others—it was safer to travel together. So we started to make our way to Bangladesh.

We knew that Bangladesh was our neighboring country and that it is Muslim.

If we stayed in Myanmar, we knew we would die. We didn't know what to expect in Bangladesh, but at least we had a chance to live.

———————

Our group made a path through the jungle and only traveled at night. If we walked during the day, we would have been killed.

So daytime was for resting. At nighttime, we walked.

I carried my two-year-old son on my shoulders. It was too hard for him to keep up. At one point, my husband got very sick. Along the way, we passed many bodies—Rohingya who had been shot or hacked to death by the extremist Buddhists who wanted us out. I tried to protect my son from seeing these things by covering his eyes, but I could not shield my daughters. Death was everywhere. We had no choice but to keep moving, or else we might be next.

After nine days, we finally made it to the border and crossed a river into Bangladesh. A Bangladeshi man took us on his boat for a fee. The boat was small—it could fit only ten people at a time—and it had no motor, so he had to row. Thankfully, my family stayed together. We were all so scared because none of us could swim. It took four hours to reach the other side.

When we arrived in Bangladesh, I fought back tears. We had made it. The threat of the genocide was behind us. It took us three hours to walk to the camp. There were so many Rohingya fleeing that we just followed everyone else. We were a crowd of strangers marching together toward a common unknown destination. But the relief I felt did not erase the fear. I had no idea what to expect in this next phase.

When we arrived, this is what we found: a big, open space and too many people—more than eight thousand came the same month that we did to join camps that were already overcrowded. Our first night, we slept under a plastic sheet. Eventually, my family received a tent, but then the monsoons came, and there was concern that the area where we had set up our camp would be flooded, so my family and hundreds of others were all moved to another camp.

This new camp is accessible only by walking up a mountain—there is no road. The closest road is a thirty-minute walk. This area, where we have built a hut out of bamboo, is extremely windy and exposed to the elements. We are stuck here because Bangladesh does not allow the

Rohingya to leave these camps. If we tried, we would be arrested and returned to the camps. So it is pointless.

We are doing the best we can. The Bangladeshi government gives us rice and lentils, so I made my own stove out of clay; I could at least cook food for my family. My mother taught me how to do this—and it brings me a small comfort to do something familiar in this place. While the conditions here are difficult, at least my husband and I have jobs. When the Love Army learned that I was making stoves, they hired me to build them to give to other refugees as gifts. I have since made more than two thousand stoves. My husband also got a job on the cleaning team through the Love Army. Life here is hard. My children go to a temporary learning center, but you can't call it school because there are no books. They miss their home, and my oldest daughter misses our cat. She is having the hardest time. She was only seven when we escaped but old enough to understand why.

Does the world know that Rohingya have been suffering genocide for a long time? Do they understand why? Can anyone help us?

I understand that the Bangladeshi government wants us to return to Myanmar, but we do not want to go. There is nothing left there for us except sadness. My people are here.

At this camp. They share my story and my pain. They know me. Why would I leave?

The only way I could ever return to my home is if my family was guaranteed to be treated with dignity. My question is, when will that be?

Farah

This Was My Story

•

Uganda → Canada

The first time I met Farah was at a job interview. She was one of a handful of women we were talking with to be the new CEO of Malala Fund. After she was hired, I joked with her that I liked her because she was nearly as short as I am. But, of course, the reason I liked her was that she is smart, she had good nonprofit experience as well as having worked in government, and she believes in the cause of girls' education as much as I do. She also has a quiet strength that I responded to.

I didn't know at the time that Farah was also a refugee—she is a Canadian born in Uganda with an Indian family background. She rarely talks about her background, but hers is an important story. The refugee stories we often see are those of people who are still in danger, who are still struggling. We assume that once they've found a new home, that's the end of the story. Often, it's the beginning of a new story.

Learning about Farah's background made me wonder how many refugees who have started over hesitate to tell their stories. It made me really think about how you can look at a person but not even begin to know the first thing about them. And now as I meet displaced families with young children, I wonder how those kids will grow up and what they will be told.

Farah, like so many young displaced people, grew up with a weight on her shoulders she didn't fully understand, and now we work together every day to help others rise up from under the weight they carry.

resilience

—Malala

I buckled myself into the seat of my flight leaving Tanzania for Entebbe, Uganda. The plane was packed—or maybe it only felt that way because it was a small plane. Thankfully, I had a window seat. I don't recall whether the plane was full of tourists or citizens. I do know that despite being born in Uganda, I did not feel like either one. I must have looked nervous, because the guy beside me asked me if I was okay. I nodded and thanked him.

I closed my eyes and just breathed, an attempt to quiet my racing heart. I *was* nervous, maybe even a little scared. I was thirty-six years old, and it was my first trip back to the place where I was born—and forced to flee.

That was 1972. This was 2006, and I had just said goodbye to one of my best friends after climbing Mount Kilimanjaro together the day before. It had been a transformative experience for us both. She was heading back to Canada, the only place I had ever called home. I, however, was heading to Uganda, my birthplace, of which I had no memory.

I was two years old when my parents fled Kampala with me and my older sister, Amina. She was three and a half. I don't remember anything about the actual departure or the plane ride that took us almost seven thousand miles to our new home. And my parents never spoke to us about it. In fact, until I was in my twenties, I did not even understand why they had left in the first place. All I knew as a child was that we were from "away," meaning, I was not born in Canada.

It's not that my parents weren't proud of being Ugandan. They were and remain very proud. I knew that meant you ate *matoke*, a type of plantain, on Sundays with curry, as well as *paya*, a stew made from the feet of goats. We never denied that we were Muslim or Africans with Indian heritage. None of that. But the one thing I didn't truly understand until I was at university was how or why we ended up in Canada. My parents never used the word *refugee* to describe us. In fact, the word was almost never used in our home.

I knew something terrible had happened, something my parents never spoke about. I also knew my mom was sad about it. I knew she and my dad missed what they had in their old life, but I didn't know the story behind it. My parents had tried to protect me and my sister from all the tragedy as well as the politics.

But if you listened to the grown-ups during our family get-togethers—which I did—you could catch glimpses.

One thing I knew: My family did not leave Uganda by choice.

───────────

From a young age, it was clear to me that I did not fit in.

I can't tell you how many times strangers, mostly kids older than me, called me a Paki when I was young. To be honest, I did not understand what it meant. When someone explained that it was a term for a person from Pakistan, I didn't understand why it was said in a mean way. These types of derogatory comments were not one-offs. My sister and I were once called pigs, which is ironic because we are Muslims, so we don't eat pork. My father told us that pig stood for "pretty intelligent girls."

We eventually moved to Burlington, which was supposedly more diverse. But I still stood out. There, I distinctly remember a punk on his banana bike swerving up beside me to yell at me to "go back home." I still wish I'd had the nerve to yell back, "I am home."

This bullying (though we did not call it that back then)

always hurt, but not nearly as much as the time my friend, and next-door neighbor, invited me to her family's cottage for the weekend. I was excited because my parents were usually strict and overprotective; our friends were always welcome in our home, but my parents did not like the idea of our sleeping over at other people's homes. I think they saw how thrilled I was and relented.

I arrived with my friend and her father. I was so happy to be there, but then I noticed immediately how dismissive my friend's stepmother was of me. Then she said, "you people," and I realized she was talking about me. Even more humiliating, my friend's father apologized and told me she was not used to non-Canadian kids. I'd grown up in Canada. I was as Canadian as anyone else in that room. It was so uncomfortable that my friend and I left one day early.

Still to this day, if I hear anyone say "you people," my left hand starts to clench. It brings out the "how dare you?" in me.

Even though my parents spoke six languages, including Gujarati, Kutchi, Hindi, Urdu, Swahili, my first language, and English, they insisted on speaking only English with me and my sister. I now know they believed that learning the language of your host country is the best way to be accepted and begin to feel as if you belong. They did not stop there: We are Muslims, yet we celebrated Christmas, complete with a tree, presents, and turkey. This applied to Hanukkah and other non-Muslim holidays, too, because my parents embraced as much of Canadian life as they could.

I was raised to believe that we were lucky to live in Canada and that whatever we wound up doing as adults, we had to give back to the country. That was part of our value system. My parents said we were "lucky" because the Canadian government had been so welcoming to refugees from Uganda. My mom insists that she never felt like an outsider in Canada—she will tell you that people were kind, friendly, and welcoming.

I was in my first year at Queen's University (where I was on a scholarship) when I joined a Peace for Ugandans group. I don't even remember how I found this group or how they found me—it's not as if we had Facebook back then! I do remember it was headed by a black Ugandan man who was determined to arrange a trip there to help restore peace. There were maybe a dozen of us, a mix of brown and black Ugandans. When I told my parents that I was planning to return to Uganda with this group to protest corruption, poor leadership, massacres, etc., they were totally against it.

For two people who had been so supportive of every decision I had made, this shocked me. I got angry with them. That was when they finally shared with me why they left.

———————

In 1972, Idi Amin, the president of Uganda from 1971 to 1979, decided that Asian Ugandans were no longer welcome. My family's citizenship was revoked along with that of fifty thousand others. Amin's decree gave us ninety days to get out, and things changed quickly. Realizing that everything left in the bank would be seized, my mom went to the bank to get her jewelry; two soldiers followed her home.

She heard a knock on the door, and when she opened it, she saw the soldiers. They threw her down on the floor, slapped her, and stole the jewelry. As they were leaving, they threatened that if she said anything, they would kill her.

My mother was now a marked woman.

The next day, my parents went to the Canadian immigration office and put in motion their plan to leave. A few weeks later, my family left Kampala for Entebbe by bus. We were allowed one bag per person.

We arrived in Montreal at night and boarded a bus to an

army camp. There, we were offered hot chocolate, tea, and food. Then they took us to the barracks, where we slept in one room.

The next day, we were taken to Canadian immigration and told we were going to go live in a city called Saint Catharines, in Ontario.

Growing up, I didn't understand how painful it was for my parents to leave Uganda—or how much they had given up. I now know that they had come from wealthy families and had both studied in England, where my sister was born. They moved back to Kampala, where I was born, in 1970. I literally cannot imagine how stressful it must have been to be a young mother, suddenly kicked out of her home under the threat of violence, only to arrive in a country where you hardly knew anyone, nor did you know where you would live or how you would support yourself and your family, or whether you would be welcome, make friends, or find a community.

But there was no choice in the matter.

_____

I was raised to be independent and not to live in fear—but I was also raised to respect family. Even at eighteen, my parents still heavily influenced my decisions, but despite their

185

refusal to support my desire to return to Uganda with this group, I stuck with it. In the end, the group disbanded, along with any plan of going back. I remember feeling let down and thinking I would never return.

My parents were relieved. And the more I learned about what happened in Uganda—to my family and thousands of others like ours—my attitude shifted to *How did that even happen to my family, as well as an entire nation?* The older I got, the angrier I got. I began to understand why my parents protected me from the truth about where we had come from— it was too painful.

I was thirty-six when a friend dared me to climb Mount Kilimanjaro with her for charitable reasons, and I accepted. By then, I had worked for a junior cabinet minister, the minister of justice, the minister of health, and then the deputy prime minister of Canada. I was a political spokesperson during the SARS outbreak and Canada's antiterrorism response to 9/11. Imagine Farah Mohamed, Canadian government spokeswoman and herself a refugee from a part of the world that people think breeds terrorists! I was ready for a new type of challenge. I quickly realized that this trip was taking me close to my birthplace. It seemed like a sign, or at least an opportunity.

The climb was scheduled for January, and my friend had to back out because of health issues. So I called another friend and said, "What are you doing in January?" She said, "I don't know." I said, "Great, we're climbing Mount Kilimanjaro!"

That December, a month before my trip, I went to my parents and said, "I'm going back to Uganda." They were not pleased, but by then, the government had invited Ugandan exiles to come back and claim their land and help rebuild the country. My uncle Amin was there to see about the family's commercial property. My sister was planning a trip there, too.

As I said goodbye to everyone from the Kilimanjaro group and boarded the small plane to Entebbe, I felt anxious, sick to my stomach. I had my Canadian passport, which I carry everywhere I go. But I was also carrying my Ugandan citizenship card, which I had with me when I left as a two-year-old. Which of these things identified me truly?

As the plane taxied toward the Uganda airport, my worry ratcheted up, starting with *Am I going to have a problem getting*

through customs? Is my bag going to be there? The worries you
have when you're in a foreign country—but this country
should not have been foreign to me.

The customs officer was wearing a full military uniform. He said nothing to me, and I said nothing back. Usually when I go to another country, I try to learn to say *hello*
and *thank you* in the language. That was how my parents
taught me. As long as you know how to say *hello* and *thank
you* and *please*, you should be okay. I just stood there frozen.
I didn't say a thing. I didn't even make eye contact, which is
so unlike me.

When I walked through customs and saw my uncle, I
fought back tears. I was so relieved, I could feel the stress
flow out of my body.

My sister was already in Kampala. She had started working on a documentary about our family's exodus. This was
her first trip back, too, and even though she was not born
there, my sister has always had a love for Uganda. She interviewed army chiefs; she spoke to people who now live in my
parents' old house; my sister is fearless. Meanwhile, I was so
scared to be there.

That afternoon, I asked my uncle to take me to the hospital where I was born, the house where my parents lived,

and the markets where they shopped. Based on the stories my aunts and uncle had told about their childhoods, I was expecting something...grand, and maybe beautiful. But after what I saw—and I struggle to admit this—I was shocked, upset, even depressed; I had seen poverty before, but I had never seen poverty like this.

I had grown up hearing that Uganda was the pearl of Africa—that it was green and luscious and beautiful. But I saw kids standing in rubbish piles, and crumbling buildings that looked as if they had been around for centuries but no one had bothered to take care of them. All I could smell was garbage and gasoline fumes.

It all made me so sad.

I stayed a couple of days, but I did not really see anything or do anything except go visit another uncle who lived a few hours away and had a rose nursery—it was a beautiful place, but it was too late for me to enjoy it. All I could see was destruction and poverty.

When I returned home to Toronto, it was even worse. I arrived at my lovely condo, downtown, on the waterfront, and it was there that it hit me: I had spent so many years since university hating Idi Amin for denying us our country, but now, sitting on my balcony smelling fresh air, I felt guilty and thankful all at the same time.

It was a terrible thing to think that. I knew how blessed I was to live in Canada. I may not have learned about why we left Uganda until later in my life, but my parents made sure we understood how lucky we were to move to Canada. I call it refugee gratitude. But I also felt angry that one person could decide where a whole group of people could and couldn't live.

In that moment, I knew I needed to make a change. I knew that these emotions, now tapped, were not going away. I gave notice at my job and started looking for something related to the way I was feeling about Uganda. That's how I ended up working for a woman who offered me the opportunity to create a foundation in her name and to focus on the empowerment of girls in developing countries. Through that I created a program called G(irls)20 and eventually turned it into a standalone entity and began to work entirely in service to girls and young women—and this led me to Malala.

My feelings about Uganda are complicated. One-third of me remains curious and anxious to find a way to help girls in Uganda. One-third of me feels guilty that I did not grow up in Uganda. Another third is angry that the expulsion happened and that it continues to happen in places around the world. I still struggle to find out what I will do for the country where I was born. While I often feel as if my country gave up on me, I have never given up on it.

Epilogue

When I left Swat Valley, Pakistan, on October 9, 2012, my eyes were closed. I woke up a week later in the intensive care unit of a hospital in Birmingham, England. My last memories of home were of sitting on the school bus, giggling with my friend Moniba.

Even as I grew to like my new life in England, I spent years longing for home—my friends, my bedroom, my school, the sounds and smells of Mingora I had known but hadn't always appreciated. I didn't know at first that I couldn't go back. And then, when I was told, I didn't believe it. I couldn't. How was it possible that when I wasn't even conscious, I had lost my home and the world I knew so well?

It had been stolen from me by violence and terror. To remain safe, I had to stay far away from Pakistan.

Over the years, as the political climate changed, I thought maybe it was time to think about going back. We looked into it, and still the answer was no. We looked into it again, and still, no. But I was determined. I am a very stubborn person, and if there is a way, I will find it.

On March 31, 2018, I stood in my home in the Swat Valley again—and felt as if the past were reversing itself. My family and I had packed our bags and flown from England to Dubai and then from Dubai to Islamabad. We took a helicopter from Islamabad to Swat Valley. I saw the beauty of my valley for the first time in over five years from a bird's-eye view—the never-ending mountain range, the greenery, the rivers. Worried that I would lose that moment and how it made me feel, I recorded every bit in my memory and, of course, my iPhone.

I wondered if my parents had noticed this beauty as they sat beside me when I was evacuated from Swat. My father said, "We saw neither the sea nor the mountain. When your eyes were closed, our eyes were closed, too."

The air whooshed around as we landed on the same helipad where I was flown away on a stretcher. We were all silent.

Returning home was different for each of us. Atal, my youngest brother, was so young when we left. His time in Pakistan is a shadow of a memory—he's a British boy now. But for my brother Khushal and I, and our parents, the emotion we felt as we first stepped out of the helicopter and onto the earth of our valley was strong. My mother wept with joy. I took it all in. The feel of the ground, the warmth of the sun, the air that felt both foreign and familiar.

And then we did what I had dreamed about but worried would never happen again: We went home.

My heart quickened as we passed familiar landmarks—a friend's house, the streets where my brothers and I used to play, the walk to school. Soon I stood in my bedroom with my mother.

When I didn't return home from school that day in 2012, my mother wondered if I would ever see my room again, if she would ever share another quiet moment with her daughter in our home. Just seeing me standing there made my mother so happy; I could see a peace on her face I had not seen in years. Family friends live in our home now, and they were kind enough to ensure that everything in my room was as we left it. Later, my mother said, "Malala left

Pakistan with her eyes closed; now she returns with her eyes open."

And my eyes are wide open. I see how lucky I was—how lucky I am. This trip was the most exciting, memorable, beautiful, and haunting time for me and my family. Although it wasn't easy—there were several failed attempts and big disappointments—I was able to return home, however briefly. I was given the chance some will never have. For many of the young women in this book, their stories are still unfolding. Returning home for them probably feels impossible, and maybe it is. But if it's what they want, I hope that they will.

Besides our home, we had not seen our friends and family for such a long time. More than five hundred of our friends and relatives came to see us in Islamabad to greet us with hugs and prayers. We took so many pictures, and I love looking at them now that I'm back in the UK. But my greatest hope is that it will not be another five and a half years before I see their faces again.

Pakistan has changed since I left. Population growth has led to congestion in some areas. There are many more houses and people in Swat than there were in 2012. But there is also more peace. I stood on the side of a hill and looked across at the mountains where the Taliban once headquartered their forces in our area. Now there are only trees and green fields.

Still, there is much work to do in my country—although I don't live there, it is still my country. It is never far from my thoughts or actions. My dream is to see all Pakistani children have access to twelve years of free, safe, and quality education and working to build a great future for our country. And in just a few years, Malala Fund has invested heavily in girls' education in Pakistan, from opening the first secondary school for girls in Shangla to supporting girls' education activists across the country.

I didn't leave my country by choice, but I did return by choice. Having such a life-changing choice taken away from me has made me extra sensitive to the choices I have. I choose to speak out. I choose to advocate for others. I choose to accept the support of people from all over the world.

I was displaced, and I choose to use the memories of that time in my life to help me connect with the 68.5 million refugees and displaced persons around the world. To see them, to help them, to share their stories.

Afterword

October 2020

In the time since *We Are Displaced* was first published, the world has undergone a massive shift. As I write this, in October 2020, we are gripped by a global pandemic that has changed the way we live our lives. When it began, I was in my final term at Oxford, living in the halls of residence and looking forward to graduating and celebrating with my friends. But that is not how this year played out—for me, or for anyone.

When I left Oxford in March, I had been expecting to go back, to be able to walk in the beautiful gardens and study in the ancient libraries. Instead, I took classes over Zoom and completed final exams in my bedroom, with my parents and brothers scattered beyond my door throughout our home. I graduated in our backyard.

We have all had the rug pulled out from under us—our lives changed practically overnight. But my generation is more prepared. We have grown up in this broken world. We watched while those in power failed to protect refugees and religious minorities, stop attacks on schools, ensure justice for Black and minority people, or even acknowledge that climate change exists.

We have long understood that a lot of work will fall on our shoulders. Young people, especially girls, have always had to fight for change, for protection, for equity. Greta Thunberg was fifteen years old when she began her protest to get her government to pay attention to climate change. I was eleven when I started advocating for girls' education in Pakistan—and fifteen when the Taliban tried to kill me for speaking out. Marie Claire was twenty when she told her story to members of the UN to encourage them to invest in girls' education around the world. Muzoon was supposed to enter ninth grade when her family was displaced and she began encouraging girls at the Zaatari camp in Jordan to attend school.

What we all have in common is that our normal lives were taken from us, and we had to find a new way of existing—a situation that people around the world might now be able to relate to a little more than they could last year. And we will likely be the ones to lead the charge to fix what's broken.

For this afterword, I'd originally planned to focus on how between the time *We Are Displaced* was first published and now, the number of displaced persons worldwide has increased from 68.5 million to 79.5 million. I was going to convey my concern that we are headed in the wrong direction. And I was going to highlight the strength of the young women in this book as proof of our resilience in the face of so many struggles. All of that is still true, but now I will add that the global refugee crisis is one sign among many— climate change, the pandemic, lack of access to education, poverty—that our world is calling out for help and change and hope.

It is the younger generation, and girls and women like the ones featured in this book, who are answering.

Author's Note

The proceeds from *We Are Displaced* will be used to support Malala Fund's work for girls' education. Each girl and young woman* profiled in these pages has received an honorarium for sharing their stories with Malala and the readers of this book.

---

* Neither Farah nor Jennifer received honoraria for their contributions.

Acknowledgments

This book was not one I had planned to write—but current events made it impossible not to. Many people around the world have supported me and my cause, and I am grateful that my voice carries so far.

First and foremost, I am honored that these girls and women have shared their stories with me and allowed me to share them with you. I have learned the power of storytelling through my activism and my previous books, and to be able to tell their stories along with mine is a gift.

This book is made of many different parts, and a lot of people helped put it all together:

Philippa Lei, Farah Mohamed, Hannah Orenstein, Maria

Qanita, Bhumika Regmi, Taylor Royle, Tess Thomas, McKinley Tretler, and the entire Malala Fund team present and past (including Eason Jordan, Meighan Stone, and Shiza Shahid).

Malala Fund's partners who facilitated our work with many of the girls in this book: Amira Abdelkhalek, Holly Carter, Anne Dolan, Stephanie Gromek, Susan Hoenig, and Jérôme Jarre (and Muhammed Zubair).

Liz Welch, who helped get all the stories onto the page, no matter what time of day or night it was in her time zone.

Farrin Jacobs, who wanted to publish this book as much as I did. Thank you for giving so much of your time and dedication.

Karolina Sutton, my literary agent, who is small but mighty.

Megan Tingley, Katharine McAnarney, Sasha Illing-worth, Jen Graham, and the rest of the team at Little, Brown Books for Young Readers; David Shelley, Jenny Lord, Katie Espiner, Sarah Benton, Helen Richardson, Tom Noble, Katie Moss, and Holly Harley at Orion Books; Tanya Malott and Brandon Stanton.

I am lucky to have a supportive family, without whom I never would've had the courage to speak up in the first place.

The people I have met in the UK have shown me such kindness—from doctors to teachers to all of my friends—and helped me settle into this country.

My family and I were fortunate enough to be welcomed into homes when we were displaced within Pakistan, and we were not alone: Residents of the surrounding areas opened their doors to hundreds of thousands of people forced to flee. The people who hosted IDPs from Swat and the people, like Jennifer and Farah, who are supporting refugees and displaced persons now represent the best of humanity. I am grateful to them, and I am grateful to you for picking up this book and making sure that the stories of Zaynab, Sabreen, Muzoon, Najla, María, Analisa, Marie Claire, Ajida, and Farah will not be overlooked.

How You Can Help

The statistics are overwhelming. According to the most recent figures from the UNHCR, more than 44,000 people a day are forced to flee their homes, and 68.5 million people are displaced worldwide. Of those, 40 million are internally displaced, and 25.4 million are refugees. More than half of those 25.4 million refugees come from three countries: South Sudan, Afghanistan, and Syria.

Global displacement is, unfortunately, not a new phenomenon. But we are currently experiencing the biggest refugee crisis in history. Not since World War II, when more than 50 million people across Europe were displaced by violence, have so many people been forced out of their homes and countries. Since then, millions have faced similar crises, in situations you may or may not have been aware of.

So what can you do about any of this? You can start by educating yourself. There are many resources online, including trusted news sources and the website of the UNHCR (unhcr .org), that provide not only data but also context. Organizations such as International Rescue Committee (IRC),* the United Nations International Children's Emergency Fund (UNICEF), the Tent Partnership for Refugees, and Kids in Need of Defense (KIND, a US-based organization) are set up to help people from countries suffering through humanitarian crises.

You can help by donating money, of course, but also by giving time and attention. Research organizations in your community, like Jennifer did, or start a campaign of your own, like Jérôme. Volunteer, write letters to raise awareness, join or start a group to support refugees in a particular region, be kind to a new student who has been displaced and is starting over. Do what you can. Know that empathy is key. And that acts of generosity both big and small make a difference and help the world heal from its wounds.

---

* The history of the IRC dates back to Albert Einstein, who left Nazi Germany and in 1933 requested the founding of an organization to support other German refugees. "I am almost ashamed to be living in such peace while all the rest struggle and suffer," he wrote around that time. The organization, called the International Relief Association, later turned into the IRC.

About the Contributors

Zaynab is an Immigrant & Refugee Youth Ambassador with Green Card Voices and is on the honor roll as a junior at St. Catherine University, studying PIP (political science, international relations, and philosophy). She plans to be an international human-rights lawyer and to return to Yemen after finishing her law degree. Her dream is to make the world a peaceful place through law, advocacy, and social justice.

Sabreen and her husband live in Belgium and just had their baby boy, Zidane, named after the famous soccer player Zinedine Zidane. She is studying Dutch and hopes to go back to school so she can be an educated mom who can support herself and her son. She considers Belgium her new home and has no plans to return to Yemen and the life she had to run away from.

Muzoon lives in the UK, where she has been resettled with her family. She started her campaign for children's education while living in the refugee camps in Jordan, where she met Malala, and she has since become the youngest UNICEF Goodwill Ambassador and the first refugee ever appointed. When she's not traveling the world to speak out for every child's right to education, she is studying international politics at a university in the UK.

Najla lives in a settlement camp in Shariya, in the Dohuk province of Iraq, with her family and eighteen thousand other displaced people. While there is a school on-site, Najla is unable to attend because at age twenty-one, she is too old. Studying in nearby Mosul would be too dangerous, due to violence and unrest. It is her dream to go to college, ideally abroad. In the meantime, she and her sister plan to open a hair salon in Shariya.

María lives in Manuela Beltrán, Colombia, with her mom and her eighteen-year-old brother. She used to work at a nail salon but quit because she said they weren't paying her fairly. She wants to go to college to study either communications or early-childhood education because she sees that as the best way to keep her family safe. Her dream is to secure a career that would help support her and her mother so that they never have to experience hunger or poverty again.

Analisa lives with her half brother and his family in Massachusetts. She is in eleventh grade and plans to go to college to study nursing after she graduates in 2020. Her dream is to become a nurse practitioner, so she can help other people when they most need it.

Marie Claire attends Washington Adventist University in Takoma Park, Maryland, just outside Washington, DC, where she is studying nursing. Her dream is to work with the global Sigma nursing program at the United Nations, which would hopefully give her the opportunity to work with refugees worldwide, and in Zambia particularly. She wants to work as a medical practitioner and mentor, to give others hope that they, too, can follow their dreams.

Jennifer lives in Lancaster, Pennsylvania, with her husband and two sons. Seventeen members of Marie Claire's family live nearby and are all considered part of Jennifer's family. She remains an active volunteer with Church World Service, the organization that connected her with Marie Claire and her family.

Ajida lives in the Ghumdhum area of the Cox's Bazar refugee camp in Bangladesh with her husband and three children. They are five of the more than 700,000 Rohingya refugees living in this camp. As employees of the Love Army, Ajida makes clay stoves for fellow refugees, and her husband works with a cleaning crew. Their three children, ages nine, seven, and four, go to a community center, but there is no adequate school available to them. Ajida has no plans to return to her country.

Farah is of Indian heritage, born in Uganda, raised in Canada, and now resides in London, where she is the chief executive officer of Malala Fund. Malala Fund's mission is to help create a world where every girl has access to twelve years of free, safe, and quality education. Over the course of her career, she has won many awards for public service and for her commitment to empower girls and women. Her greatest adventure has been summiting Mount Kilimanjaro.

About the Author

Malala Yousafzai is a cofounder and board member of Malala Fund. Malala began her campaign for education at age eleven, when she anonymously blogged for BBC Urdu about life under the Taliban in Pakistan's Swat Valley. Inspired by her father's activism, Malala soon began advocating publicly for girls' education, attracting international media attention and awards. At age fifteen, she was attacked by the Taliban for speaking out. Malala recovered in the United Kingdom and continued her fight for girls. In 2013, she founded Malala Fund with her father, Ziauddin. A year later, Malala received the Nobel Peace Prize in recognition of her efforts to see every girl complete twelve years of free, safe, and quality education. She is currently a student at Oxford University, pursuing a degree in philosophy, politics, and economics.